PROHIBITION

The Rise and Fall of the Temperance Movement

MOVEMENTS and MOMENTS THAT CHANGED AMERICA

PROHIBITION

The Rise and Fall of the Temperance Movement

ROSEN PUBLISHING

Richard Worth

Published in 2021 by The Rosen Publishing Group, Inc.
29 East 21st Street, New York, NY 10010

Library of Congress Cataloging-in-Publication Data

Names: Worth, Richard, author.
Title: Prohibition : the rise and fall of the temperance movement / Richard Worth.
Description: New York : Rosen Publishing, 2021. | Series: Movements and moments that changed america | Includes bibliographical references and index. | Audience: Grades 6-12.
Identifiers: LCCN 2019009511 | ISBN 9781725342095 (library bound) | ISBN 9781725342088 (pbk.)
Subjects: LCSH: Prohibition—United States—Juvenile literature. | Temperance—United States—History—Juvenile literature. | United States—History—1919-1933—Juvenile literature.
Classification: LCC HV5089 .W8949 2021 | DDC 364.1/73097309041—dc23
LC record available at https://lccn.loc.gov/2019009511

Portions of this book originally appeared in *Teetotalers and Saloon Smashers: The Temperance Movement and Prohibition.*

Photo Credits: Cover, p. 3 Everett Historical/Shutterstock.com; p. 7 Authenticated News/Archive Photos/Getty Images; pp. 10–11, 98, 110–111 Bettmann/Getty Images; p. 15 Chronicle/Alamy Stock Photo; pp. 20–21 Topical Press Agency/Hulton Archive/Getty Images; p. 24 MPI/Archive Photos/Getty Images; p. 27 Private Collection/Bridgeman Images; pp. 30–31 Copyright © North Wind Picture Archives; pp. 37, 44, 65, 68–69, 73, 76–77, 83 Library of Congress Prints and Photographs Division; pp. 40–41 Fotosearch/Archive Photos/Getty Images; pp. 50–51 Chicago History Museumf/Archive Photos/Getty Images; p. 57 Library of Congress/Corbis Historical/Getty Images; p. 58 pp. 26–27 Author Internet Archive Book Images/Wikimedia Commons/File: Diocletian 'Dio' Lewis, physician and gymnastics instructor.jpg/Public Domain Mark; p. 61 Hulton Archive/Getty Images; p. 86 Enslow Publishing; pp. 90–91 Buyenlarge/Archive Photos/Getty Images; pp. 94–95 Margaret Bourke-White/The LIFE Images Collection/Getty Images; pp. 102–103, 108 Keystone-France/Gamma-Keystone/Getty Images; p. 112 Keystone/Hulton Archive/Getty Images; p. 113 guentermanaus/Shutterstock.com; p. 115 Monkey Business Images/Shutterstock.com; cover and interior pages banner graphic stockish/Shutterstock.com.

CPSIA Compliance Information: Batch #BSR20. For further information contact Rosen Publishing, New York, New York at 1-800-237-9932.

CONTENTS

Introduction 6

CHAPTER 1
Leading a Revolution 9

CHAPTER 2
Drinking Traditions 26

CHAPTER 3
The New Temperance Movement 43

CHAPTER 4
Women Take the Lead 60

CHAPTER 5
The Anti-Saloon League 72

CHAPTER 6
The Perils and the Promise of Prohibition 89

CHAPTER 7
After Prohibition 106

Conclusion 114

Chronology 117

Chapter Notes 119

Glossary 124

Further Information 125

Index 126

INTRODUCTION

Time and again, grassroots political movements have changed the course of American history. During the eighteenth century, the revolutionary uprising against Great Britain began as a grassroots movement. In Boston, the Sons of Liberty were largely average working people who finally decided that the British Parliament had pushed them too far and taxed them too much. In 1774, they stormed Boston Harbor, threw the British tea into the water, refused to pay the tea tax, and defied Parliament to stop them. A year later, the minutemen who fought at the Battles of Lexington and Concord were farmers and shopkeepers who rose up to protect what they saw as their inalienable rights. Eventually, their movement created a revolution that drove out the British rulers.

The abolition movement of the nineteenth century began as a grassroots movement to put an end to slavery. It started with a relative handful of people who were criticized as radicals for trying to outlaw slavery. As time went on, however, more and more Northerners joined the movement, helping African Americans escape bondage in the South through the Underground Railroad. The movement produced a gifted writer, Harriet Beecher Stowe, who helped turn slavery into a burning national issue with her novel *Uncle Tom's Cabin.* Those opposed to slavery created a new political party, the Republicans; elected a president, Abraham Lincoln; and eventually helped lead America during the Civil War to the abolition of slavery across the United States.

After the Civil War ended, another grassroots movement arose. This one was led primarily by women. Although they were not permitted to vote, this did not stop them from

This engraving shows a mob of women destroying barrels of alcohol in Fredericktown, Ohio, in 1879. Women may not have been able to escape domestic violence brought about by their husbands' alcoholism, but they did have the power to protest against the manufacture and sale of alcohol.

taking to the streets and lobbying state legislators to sound the alarm about the evils of alcohol. Some of them were married to men who stopped at taverns after work and spent their paychecks on drink. Later they arrived home drunk and beat their wives and children. As the Prohibition movement grew, it captured the attention of state legislators. Gradually, the Prohibitionists gained enough support to force legislators into passing prohibition laws.

Together with the Anti-Saloon League, also led by women as well as a few men, the Prohibitionists became one of America's most successful lobbying efforts. They helped elect congressmen who supported their movement and eventually won a majority in Congress who proposed a prohibition amendment to the US Constitution. By 1919, a majority of states had approved the amendment, and it became law.

1

LEADING A REVOLUTION

Revolutionary leaders can come from almost anywhere. They might be politicians, members of the clergy, or well-known actors or artists. But they can also emerge from nowhere, becoming famous almost overnight for a revolutionary act that stuns society.

In the early morning of a warm June day in 1900, a gray-haired grandmother appeared at the door of John Dobson's tavern in Kiowa, Kansas. She was dressed in black. The 6-foot-tall (183-centimeter-tall) woman with a frown set above her square jaw entered the "joint," as she called it. She carried some small items from her home in Medicine Lodge, about 10 miles (16 kilometers) away.

Once inside, she began hurling these items at glassware, liquor bottles, mirrors, and windows. She shattered everything in sight. After completing her work at Dobson's, the woman went along the street to other taverns and saloons. At these taverns, she picked up billiard balls and cue sticks. She used them to repeat the work she had begun at Dobson's. The woman said that a voice in a dream had persuaded her to go to Kiowa. The voice had said, "Take something in your hands, and throw at these places in Kiowa and smash them."[1] Eventually, the local sheriff stopped

Carry Nation acted as a catalyst in the effort to outlaw the use of alcohol, and her dynamic leadership brought many women out on the streets and in front of state legislatures to support the passage of prohibition laws.

the woman from entering any other saloons. But instead of throwing her in jail, he decided to let her off with a warning.

Carry Nation had begun her campaign of destruction against the saloons of Kansas. It was her battle for temperance, a largely religious effort to get people to stop drinking alcohol. In 1880, the Kansas legislature had passed a law calling for prohibition, outlawing the use of alcohol. But the Kansas courts and the local sheriffs had ignored the law. They let the saloons remain open. In mid-June, Nation appeared at a meeting of the local chapter of the Woman's Christian Temperance Union (WCTU). This was a national organization committed to reducing the amount of drinking and passing prohibition laws. Nation was president of the group.

On a wintry day in late December 1900, she traveled to Wichita, Kansas. The next morning, Nation appeared at the Carey Hotel bar. This was the fanciest bar in the city. Nation later called herself "the right arm of God . . . destined to wreck every saloon in your city."[2] She believed that God had chosen her to destroy the saloons and put an end to the influence of alcohol.

Years earlier, her husband had died from alcoholism. Nation knew that many other women suffered as she had from the influence of alcohol. Their husbands got drunk at bars. They spent much of the money that was necessary to support their families, and then they came home and beat their wives.

At the Carey Hotel bar, Nation did about three thousand dollars worth of damage. The chief of police hauled her off to jail. While in prison, she wrote letters describing her mission. Some of the men who had encountered Nation in the saloons actually admired her work. These men called her "Mother Nation" because of the warmth and sympathy she showed them—even while she was destroying their saloons. Eventually, Mother Nation was released on bail. She had no plans to stop her work.

Later in January 1901, she continued to destroy the saloons of Wichita. This time, Nation was joined by other women who believed in her temperance crusade. Nation used a hatchet to destroy furniture and smash bottles in each saloon that she entered. Jailed and released again, she finally left Wichita after a mob threatened to lynch her, or kill her without a trial.

Joining the Movement

From Wichita, Nation took the train to Enterprise, Kansas. Local women had invited her to come to their town to continue her work. At Enterprise, she greeted a crowd of supporters. They included the mother of the town's mayor. Nation immediately went to work, continuing her "hatchetation," as she called it. Accompanied by a large

The Words of Carry Nation

Carry Nation's tirades against alcohol and those who drank it were often flowery and poetic. Here are examples of some of her more memorable lines:

"You have put me in here a cub, but I will come out roaring like a lion...."

"Who hath sorrow? Who hath woe?/They who do not answer no;/They whose feet to sin incline/While they tarry at the wine."

"I felt invincible. My strength was that of a giant. God was certainly standing by me. I smashed five saloons with rocks before I ever took a hatchet."

"Men are nicotine soaked, beer besmirched, whiskey-greased, red-eyed devils."[3]

crowd, she went into a saloon owned by John Schilling and smashed the items inside. That evening she spoke to a large group of supporters in the street. Schilling's wife, Belle, stepped out of the crowd and punched Nation in the eye. It was her way of paying back the woman who had destroyed her husband's livelihood.

When Nation tried to smash up another saloon the next day, John Schilling and four female prostitutes stopped her. According to historian Fran Grace, Schilling held Nation while the women "beat and whipped her." Soon afterward, Nation left town.[4]

Nevertheless, Carry Nation's crusade was gathering momentum. People in Kansas were comparing her to the famous abolitionist John Brown. He had used violent means to try to end slavery. Almost half a century earlier, Kansas had become a bloody battleground between abolitionists and slaveholders. Each side tried to take control of Kansas. To drive out the proslavery forces, Brown and his sons murdered five slaveholders in 1855. Four years later, Brown led a small group of armed men that captured the United States arsenal at Harper's Ferry, Virginia. He hoped to use the weapons at the arsenal to begin a slave uprising in the South. Brown was captured and later hanged. But he was hailed as a martyr by many abolitionists in the North.

By 1900, Nation was being called the "John Brown of Prohibition" by her supporters. Soon, other people in Kansas marched into the streets, destroying saloons. But these Kansans were in a minority. Throughout the rest of the United States, many people thought that Nation had gone much too far. They thought she was crazy because of her extreme action against saloons.

Even Kansans were divided over their attitudes toward Nation. In January 1901, she appeared at a convention of the Kansas State Temperance Union. Among the delegates were many of her supporters. Some of them contributed money to present Nation with a medal. It bore the words "The Bravest Woman in Kansas." More moderate members of the convention, however, thought that she had gone too far with her tactics. Among them was twenty-four-year-old Madeline Southard. After the meeting, she spoke with Nation. Southard was won over and changed her mind. She

This artwork depicts Carry Nation and her followers destroying a bar in Kansas City.

joined Carry Nation's Home Defenders Army, a group of men and women dedicated to destroying the saloons. They wanted to force Kansans to abide by the prohibition law.

A majority of Americans pointed out that the Home Defenders were taking the law into their own hands. But members of the organization regarded themselves as defenders of the Kansas prohibition law. Many Kansans had become discouraged that the law would never be enforced. In fact, support was growing to repeal it. As Fran Grace wrote, "[Nation's] hatchet empowered Kansas prohibitionists to believe that God was still on their side and that God would not allow the wets [supporters of drinking] to take over their alcohol-free promised land."[5]

The Home Defenders' opponents, however, felt entitled to drink in saloons, or dram shops as they were called. These opinions did not stop Nation and her army. In February, Nation, accompanied by Southard and others, entered the Senate Bar in Topeka. There, the "smashers" destroyed kegs of beer. Nation herself heaved a cash register through the air, which broke into pieces upon impact.

Nation planned to take her dry crusade to other towns. Before leaving Topeka, she had preached to large crowds about the evils of alcohol. As Nation put it, "A woman is stripped of everything by [saloons]. Her husband is torn from her; she is robbed of her sons, her home, her food, and her virtue. . . . Truly does the saloon make a woman bare of all things!"[6]

Someone had suggested that Nation adopt as her symbol a little metal hatchet. Nation ordered hatchet pins to be manufactured so she could sell them to her supporters. These helped to finance her campaign. From Topeka, Nation traveled to Kansas City, Missouri; Des Moines, Iowa;

and Chicago, Illinois. Addressing a large crowd in Chicago, Nation read Psalm 144 from the Bible.

Nation's Early Years

Carry Nation's temperance crusade arose from the early experiences of her life. Carrie Amelia Moore was born in Kentucky on November 25, 1846. (She alternately called herself "Carrie" and "Carry." She finally adopted "Carry" when she led the temperance crusade.) Her father, George Moore, was a wealthy farmer and slave owner. Carrie was very close to her father. He was a tall man with a full beard and a corncob pipe constantly stuck in his mouth. About a decade later, the Moore family moved to Missouri. They were a strongly religious family. When she was still a child, Carrie was baptized by the local minister who dunked her in a stream.

Just across the border from their farm, Kansas was erupting in violence over the issue of slavery. That violence would eventually spread across the nation. In December 1860 and in early 1861, Southern states seceded from the Union and formed the Confederate States of America. In April, Confederate soldiers bombarded the Union stronghold at Fort Sumter in South Carolina. This began the Civil War. The Moore family left for Texas. They wanted to keep their slaves and hoped to find safety from the war. But along the way, many of their slaves died. Moore eventually took his family back to Missouri. He had lost a lot of money.

By the time the Civil War ended in 1865, the Moores were living on a farm in southern Missouri. Boarding with them was a twenty-five-year-old man named Charles Gloyd. A handsome young man with a mustache and a goatee, Gloyd was a teacher and a doctor. He had treated wounded soldiers in the Union Army during the Civil War. After the war, he came to Missouri and began instructing students. Carrie was attracted to Gloyd, but her parents opposed the marriage. Gloyd had a serious drinking problem. Nevertheless, Carrie and Gloyd continued to see each other and eventually married in 1867.

Carrie later became pregnant and gave birth to a daughter named Charlien. Her marriage was very unhappy, however, because Gloyd continued to abuse alcohol. He regularly went to a bar and remained there overnight. Gloyd died in 1869 as a result of alcoholism.

For the next seven years, Carrie remained a widow. She moved in with Gloyd's mother in Holden, Missouri, who helped Carrie raise Charlien. While living in Holden, Carrie met David Nation, a city attorney. Nation was twenty years older than Carrie. He was a bald, impressive-looking man with a full beard. His wife had died, leaving him with several children. Nation soon began courting Carrie. The couple was married in December 1877.

David Nation had been a successful lawyer and newspaper editor. He believed that there were opportunities to make more money elsewhere, however. In 1877, Nation and his family moved to Texas to run a farm. Knowing little about farming, Nation soon left Carrie to run everything. He looked for work elsewhere. The family had little money, but Carrie managed to provide enough food for the children. In 1879, she left the farm and began running the Columbia Hotel on the Brazos River in Texas. From all these experiences, Carrie Nation developed a strong sense of self-reliance. She learned to trust her own decisions and support herself, without any help from her husband. As a hotel manager, she also made many new friends. Unfortunately, one of her closest friends, Major Burke, became another victim of alcoholism.

In 1881, the Nations moved to Richmond, Texas. There, Carrie opened another hotel, the National Hotel. She also became very active in the local Richmond churches. During one gathering in Richmond, Carrie had a profound religious experience, She believed that God had selected her to do important work. She began to see herself as "Carrie Nation, chosen of God."[7]

Meanwhile, an employer had offered David Nation a new job. David became a preacher at a church in Medicine Lodge, Kansas. In 1889, Carrie gave up her work in Texas and returned to Kansas with her husband. During the 1890s, she helped the poor. She opened a school, taught local children, and brought food and clothing to poor families. Carrie Nation had not forgotten her experiences with alcoholism, which had claimed the life of her first husband. She also realized what a burden this illness placed on women who were married to alcoholic men.

During the nineteenth century, women had few rights in marriage. They were prevented by law from owning their own property. If they were successful in obtaining a divorce from an abusive husband—which was very difficult under the law—they generally lost custody of their children.

Carrie Nation joined the temperance movement, which helped women take control of their own lives. During the late nineteenth century, many Americans believed that it was unfeminine for women to join temperance groups. Men were especially critical of women who spoke at meetings. This activity, they thought, should be reserved only for men. The women who joined the Woman's Christian Temperance Union (WCTU), including Nation, disagreed.

WOMENS CHRISTIAN TEMPERANCE UNIO

Members of the Woman's Christian Temperance Union (WCTU) march on Washington, DC, wearing their white ribbons. Women were so infuriated over the effects of drinking that they violated long-standing traditions and spoke out in front of public meetings.

The Kansas Woman's Christian Temperance Union

Founded in 1878 outside Lawrence, the Kansas WCTU met a year later at its first general meeting. Their symbol was the white ribbon, the same one that had been adopted by the national WCTU founded several years earlier. The Kansas WCTU played an active role in the adoption of a prohibition law in Kansas during 1879 and 1880. From there, the organization advocated for a law to require that temperance become part of the curriculum in church Sunday schools, which was passed in 1885. The organization supported other causes beyond temperance, including women's suffrage, prison reform, and anticigarette legislation. The Kansas WCTU was organized hierarchically, that is, local unions in towns, a county-wide union made up of representatives from the local unions, and finally the state WCTU. In addition, the Kansas WCTU produced a regular publication called *Our Messenger,* as well as unions for young people, beginning at age six.

Nation spoke at local meetings of the Kansas WCTU. This organization was founded in 1878. She also supported women's suffrage, the right to vote. Except in the territory of Wyoming, this right was granted only to adult males. She believed that with the vote, women would change the laws and enact prohibition.

In terms of women's rights, Kansas was ahead of the rest of the United States. Under pressure from the WCTU, a law that let women vote in city elections had been passed in 1887. The WCTU also successfully lobbied the state legislature, which passed a law in 1889 banning the sale of tobacco to children. It was only nine years earlier that the Kansas legislature had passed a prohibition law. In Medicine Lodge, Nation addressed groups of schoolchildren and told them not to drink alcohol when they became adults.

Nevertheless, the work of the WCTU did not seem to have an impact on alcohol consumption. Authorities did not enforce the prohibition law that had been passed by the legislature. Nation and other women, therefore, turned to different tactics. They sang hymns in front of saloons. They hoped to persuade the men inside to leave the bars and return home. In addition to saloons, pharmacies were targeted by the WCTU. These stores sold medicines that contained large amounts of alcohol. Some pharmacies also stocked large barrels of whiskey, which they sold to customers.

On December 11, 1894, Nation, who soon began spelling her first name as "Carry," took the first action that eventually led to her hatchetation in Wichita. Along with three other women, she approached a pharmacy owned by O. L. Day in Medicine Lodge. One of the women carried a sledgehammer. Nation entered the pharmacy ahead of

Some women thought that the best way to stop their husbands, fathers, and brothers from drinking in saloons was to shame them into abstinence by singing hymns outside the doors.

the other women. They included the president of the local WCTU, Kate Cain. Nation demanded to be told whether the pharmacist was selling whiskey. When he refused her request, she looked at a whiskey barrel and said, "Women, this is whiskey!"[8] The local police arrived and tried to stop the women. But Nation and the others got the whiskey barrel outside and destroyed it.

Over the next few years, Carry Nation continued her work. She preached against alcohol and helped the poor. She and her husband spent three years in Oklahoma Territory, before returning to Kansas in 1899. There her temperance crusade moved into high gear. Its roots lay in Nation's religious beliefs and the personal losses she had endured from alcohol. Many other women had similar experiences. They also shared her desire to speak out on important issues. They wanted to assert their independence and achieve greater political power in the United States. However, some of them disagreed with Nation's approach, believing she went too far with her hatchetation.

Nevertheless, all of these women, and men as well, came together in the temperance movement. Its origins lay in the early years of the United States. But the movement would catch fire in the late nineteenth century and change the history of America.

2

DRINKING TRADITIONS

The Pilgrims have an important place in American history because of their long, dangerous trip to the New World in 1620. They established a new religion in Massachusetts and set a standard for New England independence. But the Pilgrims should also be remembered for something else.

Among their most precious cargo on the Mayflower were kegs of beer. On the long voyage across the stormy Atlantic Ocean, the settlers relied on beer to quench their thirst. The alcohol contained in beer preserved much of its freshness, unlike water. Indeed, many Europeans were reluctant to drink water. It was often polluted and carried deadly diseases. Instead, the Pilgrims relied on dark beer. As they reached Plymouth, however, the supply of beer was running low. The crew of the Mayflower wanted to preserve what was left for their return trip to England. Nevertheless, they finally agreed to share their beer rations with the Pilgrims. When the supply was finally exhausted, the Pilgrims were forced to drink water from the streams they found in Massachusetts. To their surprise, the water was clean and fresh.

Although they were happy to find drinkable water, the Massachusetts colonists did not suddenly lose their taste for

American artist Howard Pyle (1853–1911) created this illustration titled "The Master Caused Us to Have Some Beere," for the December 1883 issue of *Harper's Magazine.* The Pilgrims who settled in Massachusetts had strict rules of behavior that governed their lives, but that did not prevent them from drinking beer and brandy.

beer. Instead, by the 1630s, they established small breweries and opened local taverns. Women also made beer at home.

In addition to beer, the English colonists drank other types of alcohol. Brandy, imported from Europe, was much stronger than beer. Therefore, as hardy pioneers began to move westward they carried small containers of brandy with them.

Another popular drink among the colonists was rum. England founded colonies in the Caribbean during the seventeenth century. On these Caribbean islands, planters established large sugar cane plantations. African slaves worked this land. After harvesting the cane and boiling it, the slaves produced liquid molasses. This was the key ingredient in rum. The molasses was fermented and distilled. That is, the liquid was heated into a vapor. Then the vapor was cooled to produce rum. Some of the rum was light colored. But caramel could also be added to rum, turning it to a dark color.

At first, rum was shipped from the Caribbean to the English colonies in North America. It had much more alcohol in it than beer. By 1700, the colonists in New England were producing their own rum. A distillery opened in Boston to process molasses. Others followed in Newport and Providence, Rhode Island. Indeed, enterprising merchants made molasses part of a highly lucrative three-cornered trade. The Triangle Trade, as it was called, brought rum to Africa. There, the rum was bartered with local chiefs for slaves that had been captured in raids. The slaves were loaded onboard colonial ships. Then the slaves were transported to the Caribbean islands, where they were sold. Some of the money was used to purchase molasses.

In addition to sending rum to Africa, the New England distilleries sold the popular drink throughout the English colonies. As many as 600,000 gallons (2.3 million liters) were shipped annually to other parts of North America. Indeed, rum probably became the most popular alcoholic beverage in the colonies during the eighteenth century.[1]

Aside from rum, the colonists also favored other types of alcoholic drinks. Once established in new settlements, farmers laid out fields of wheat, barley, and corn. Much of their harvest was turned into food. But farmers used some of the wheat and corn to produce alcohol. Rye, wheat, corn, and other grains were mashed together into a liquid. Then the liquid was distilled into a powerful whiskey. It was sometimes called John Barleycorn. Whiskey was very popular among the Scots. As some of them immigrated to North America, they may have brought their knowledge of making whiskey with them. Some of the whiskey was known as rye. Another form of whiskey was called bourbon, because it was first produced in Bourbon, Kentucky.

Regular Drinking: A Colonial Tradition

American colonists believed that alcohol was good for them. In fact, they helped themselves to several drinks a day. Some adults began their day with a drink in the early morning soon after they awoke. A glass of rum or brandy, they believed, was a strong "morning pick-me-up." Soon afterward, colonists poured themselves rum or beer to accompany breakfast. As one colonist wrote, "I have frequently seen fathers wake their child of a year old from a sound sleep to make it drink Rum, or brandy."[2] They believed that any beverage, even distilled spirits, that

In colonial America, drinking rum, beer, and brandy was part of the daily routine for many adults who poured themselves a drink several times a day.

they thought was good for adults would also be beneficial for their children.

After breakfast, men went to work in the fields. Some also worked as craftsmen, such as blacksmiths, silversmiths, and carpenters. About eleven o'clock, each of these men put down their tools for another drink. A glass of rum or beer, they believed, helped restore their energy for the rest of the day. At lunch, during the early afternoon, many colonists went to a tavern to eat. They usually washed down their dinner with another alcoholic beverage.

After returning to work, men often stopped again when a bell rang at four o'clock in the afternoon. This was the signal for another drink. After the day was done, beer usually accompanied supper. The last thing at night, many colonists downed another glass of rum. They thought the alcohol would keep them warm during the cold winters and help them sleep. (Today, doctors know that alcohol can actually lower the body's temperature and prevents a person from getting quality sleep.)

Alcohol was not only a routine part of every day. Drinking also accompanied special events throughout the colonies, such as parties. After burying the dead, mourners drank alcohol. During local elections to colonial legislatures, politicians were expected to entertain the voters. They provided food and plenty of alcohol. This helped persuade people to vote for them so they could win elections. In 1753, an editorial in a New York newspaper complained that many voters traded their votes for "Beer and Brandy." Alcohol was widely available at polling places where Americans cast their votes. As one observer, Ferdinand Bayard, put it, "candidates offer drunkenness openly to anyone who is willing to give them his vote."[3]

George Washington produced alcohol on his estates in Virginia. In one of his fields, he grew rye that was distilled into whiskey and sold to the public. He also produced molasses beer that was served at social events at his plantation, Mount Vernon. Thomas Jefferson constructed a brewery at his plantation, Monticello. He was also an expert in fine wines, consuming three glasses of wine each day.[4] Another colonial leader, John Adams, started his day with a mug of hard (alcoholic) cider.[5]

Most Americans believed that drinking alcohol was perfectly acceptable, at least in moderation. Increase Mather, a leading clergyman in Massachusetts during the seventeenth century, expressed this opinion. In a sermon called "Wo to Drunkards," he wrote: "Drink is in itself a good creature of God, and to be received with thankfulness, but the abuse of drink is from Satan, the wine is from God, but the Drunkard is from the Devil."[6] Drunkards were not tolerated in colonial society. They were sent to jail or fined. If they continued to drink, drunkards were required to wear a red letter "D" on their clothing. Some people turned away from their heavy drinking; they were welcomed back by their friends.[7]

Drinking Habits in the Eighteenth Century

Attitudes toward drinking did not change in the years leading up to American independence. During this era, the British parliament passed a series of taxes on the colonists. One of these was the Sugar Act in 1764. This new law prohibited merchants from buying molasses in any Caribbean islands, except those owned by England. On the French-controlled islands, molasses was cheaper. Merchants were very angry over the Sugar Act. So they decided to ignore the law and smuggled in cheaper molasses to make rum.

The Sugar Act also placed a heavy tax on Madeira. This was a favorite wine of the American colonists that they imported from Portugal. The Sugar Act, along with other measures passed by the British parliament, finally convinced the American colonists to declare their independence in 1776. During the war, the British navy clamped a blockade on the North American coast. As a result, American merchants could no longer import large quantities of molasses. America's drinking habits rapidly changed. They switched from mugs of rum to glasses of whiskey. Each soldier in the Continental Army received 4 ounces (118 milliliters) of whiskey per day. American soldiers supplemented this ration by buying more liquor from merchants who did business at army campsites. Sometimes, heavy drinking led to drunken brawls among the men, and even worse. At the Battle of Eutaw Springs, North Carolina, in 1781, American soldiers captured British supply wagons. They discovered a large supply of alcohol. The soldiers stopped fighting and began drinking. Soon afterward, the British mounted a counterattack, driving the American army off the battlefield.

Nevertheless, the Continental Army eventually trapped the British at Yorktown, Virginia, in October 1781. Victory over the British redcoats in the Battle of Yorktown guaranteed American independence. During the years of the long struggle, society had changed. Men who fought for freedom believed that they were no longer required to listen to people in authority. They had not listened to the British parliament. Nor did they want to listen to local clergymen who told them how to drink. The churches

Madeira Wine

On the Portuguese islands of Madeira, the climate is ideal for planting vineyards and growing grapes to produce a wine called Madeira. When the Portuguese began the voyages of exploration in the 1500s, merchants began purchasing Madeira to sell in the new colonies of North America. By the eighteenth century, American merchants, including John Hancock, brought Madeira wine to the colonies where it had become very popular. In fact, British tax collectors took control of one of Hancock's ships, the *Liberty*, in 1768 in a disagreement over a tax on his wine. This was among the events that eventually led to the outbreak of the American Revolution. In the new American Republic, after the war, Madeira continued to be a very popular wine among the colonists. In fact, it was a special favorite among the Founding Fathers, including John Adams, Thomas Jefferson, and George Washington.

and the clergy lost much of their influence. In the years after independence, more settlers moved west, away from churches and local governments. On the frontier, men might spend many days alone, hunting or trapping. When they came back from the wilderness, some of these frontiersmen headed for the local taverns. Then they began to drink, often going on long drinking binges.

Farmers were also growing more grain and corn in their fields. Part of these crops were turned into beer and whiskey. This increased the opportunity to consume more alcohol. Before the American Revolution, each adult consumed about 6 gallons (23 L) of alcohol per year. This meant far more than 6 gallons of beer, for example, which was only 6 percent alcohol.[8] In the 1790s, the amount of alcohol that Americans drank shot up to more than 7 gallons (26 L) per year. As one observer, Samuel Dexter, put it in 1814, "the quantity of ardent spirits . . . surpasses belief."[9]

A majority of Americans believed that the amount of alcohol they drank was their own decision to make. After all, they had just fought a long war to secure their freedom. But some cultural leaders disagreed. Among them was Dr. Benjamin Rush, a leading patriot during the American Revolution. In 1772, he had published a pamphlet titled *Sermons to Gentlemen Upon Temperance and Exercise.* In 1785, Rush published another pamphlet, *An Inquiry into the Effects of Ardent Spirits on the Human Mind and Body.* In this booklet, Rush argued that alcohol could lead to uncontrolled drinking, which would hurt a person's health. He said heavy drinking was an addiction. By permitting it, he said, "Our country [would soon] be governed by men chosen by intemperate and corrupted voters."[10]

Rush mounted a campaign against heavy drinking. He sent out copies of his book to anyone who would read it. His book did not preach total abstinence from alcohol, only moderation. But he urged people to give up "ardent spirits" such as rum and whiskey, in favor of weaker alcoholic drinks such as wine.

When it came to drinking, Dr. Rush did not change the minds of many Americans. The United States remained

Dr. Benjamin Rush, a highly respected American patriot, was also one of the first to warn against the dangers of too much drinking.

a leader in the worldwide consumption of alcohol. In 1791, the secretary of the treasury, Alexander Hamilton, decided that the federal government could make money on Americans' alcohol consumption. Hamilton proposed an excise tax on whiskey. He also hoped that the tax might cut down on drinking. "The consumption of ardent spirits," he said, "is carried to an extreme which is truly to be regretted."[11]

The tax amounted to seven-and-a-half cents on each gallon (4 L) of whiskey. This angered the farmers of western Pennsylvania who made and sold whiskey. They refused to pay the tax and drove the tax collectors off their farms. The so-called Whiskey Rebellion in 1794 was an uprising over the freedom to produce alcohol without being taxed. President George Washington finally called out thirteen thousand militia, who put down the Whiskey Rebellion. The farmers began paying the whiskey tax.

A New Mission

Benjamin Rush was among the first leaders of the early temperance movement. Rush called on Americans to practice moderation. In 1789, a group of farmers in Litchfield, Connecticut, announced that they would no longer drink alcohol during breaks from work. In 1808, the Reverend Lebbeus Armstrong helped found a new group called the Union Temperance Society of Moreau and Northumberland. This was probably the first temperance society in the United States.[12]

More than forty men joined the organization. They drew up a constitution. Among other things, it stated, "No member shall drink . . . any distilled spirits . . . except by advice of a physician, or in case of actual disease; . . .

No member shall be intoxicated, under penalty of fifty cents."[13] The early temperance movement did not preach full abstinence, or giving up all alcohol consumption. The movement wanted people to drink only a little bit, such as having wine at dinners.

In 1811, the Presbyterian Church organized a temperance convention. Dr. Rush mailed copies of his book to the

The Whiskey Rebellion

In the early days of the American republic, there was such a high demand for alcoholic spirits that many wheat farmers used part of their crop to produce whiskey. It was also cheaper to transport barrels of whiskey to market than wheat. Then in 1791, the administration of President George Washington set a new tax on alcoholic spirits, including whiskey, of 6 to 18 cents per gallon. Many farmers became so angry that revolts broke out, and they refused to pay the tax. These revolts grew violent, and in western Pennsylvania, farmers burned the home of the local tax collector. In 1794, President Washington led thousands of soldiers westward to put down the rebellion. The soldiers arrested more than one hundred farmers and brought an end to the revolt. However, the tax on alcohol was not finally repealed until 1802.

The defense of the freedom to drink and make money producing alcohol led to the first armed protest in the new republic—the Whiskey Rebellion. This artwork shows a tax official being tarred and feathered by the rebellious farmers as his home burns in the background.

convention in Philadelphia. In New England and farther south, Presbyterian congregations took up the cry of temperance. They warned that children should be educated about alcohol's problems. They also said that employers should not provide their workers with alcohol on the job.

An American temperance movement was beginning.

3

THE NEW TEMPERANCE MOVEMENT

The Reverend Lyman Beecher was an evangelical minister. He believed that Christians should form a direct, close relationship with God. During the early nineteenth century, the United States was in the midst of the Second Great Awakening. Like its predecessor—the First Great Awakening of the eighteenth century—it was a massive Christian revival, involving thousands of people. Evangelical preachers held large outdoor camp meetings. There, Christian believers received the spirit of God and took a pledge to commit themselves to God's teachings. Revivalist organizations advertised the meetings in printed pamphlets and newspapers. The religious gatherings drew crowds of people who became involved in a highly emotional experience. They sang hymns, prayed with other devout believers, and pledged themselves to God.

The Second Great Awakening occurred at the same time as the growing temperance movement. In fact, temperance leaders adopted many of the same techniques. One of the earliest temperance groups was the Massachusetts Society for the Suppression of Intemperance (MSSI). It was founded in Boston in 1813. This group allowed moderate drinking

Lyman Beecher was a nationally renowned clergyman and the leader of one of America's leading families during the 1800s.

The Beecher Family

In 1825, Reverend Lyman Beecher delivered a blistering sermon to his congregation. "Intemperance is a national sin," the silver-haired clergyman told them.[1] "Who hath sorrow?" he asked them. "Who hath contentions? who hath babbling? who hath wounds without cause? who hath redness of eyes? They that tarry long at the wine!"[2] Beecher, America's best-known preacher, called on his congregation in Litchfield, Connecticut, to give up drinking. He urged them to practice abstinence. Beecher later published his words in a book called *Six Sermons on Intemperance,* and many people throughout the United States read it. Not only was Beecher famous, several of his children would become equally well known. Harriet Beecher Stowe, one of Beecher's daughters, would later publish *Uncle Tom's Cabin,* which galvanized the abolition movement. Her sister, Catharine Beecher, was a strong advocate for women's education and founded the Hartford Female Seminary in 1823 and the Western Female Institute in 1832. And Beecher's son, Henry Ward Beecher, followed in his father's footsteps and became one of America's best known clergymen.

but opposed heavy drinking. However, the MSSI did little to advertise its efforts and gained few supporters.

Another early temperance group was the American Society for the Promotion of Temperance, founded by members of the clergy in 1826. The group shortened its name to the American Temperance Society (ATS). To attract new members, the ATS published pamphlets warning people about the dangers of alcohol. At first, the ATS preached temperate drinking. But many of its members believed that temperance was not sufficient to prevent drunkenness. Eventually, a split occurred in the organization. Some members favored temperance, while the rest of the members believed in total abstinence. In 1833, ATS members defeated a proposal to support abstinence at a convention. Three years later, however, a majority voted to adopt total abstinence as the guiding principle of their group.

In fact, the origin of the word "teetotalers" arose during the early days of the temperance movement. Local groups discussed whether to insist on total abstinence or permit moderate drinking of wine and beer. Those members who favored total abstinence placed a "t" next to their names. They became known as teetotalers.

By 1833, about 1.5 million Americans had joined temperance groups. They looked to the ATS for leadership. Alcohol consumption dropped from 7 gallons (26 L) per person, annually, to just over 3 gallons (11 L) by 1840.[3] By this time, temperance groups had abandoned support of moderate drinking. They insisted that each member take a pledge of complete abstinence. Some members continued to drink moderately and decided to give up their membership. When temperance groups had permitted moderate drinking of beer and wine, brewers and wine makers supported them. With the change in direction of the temperance movement, it lost the backing of beer and wine makers.

Conflict in the Temperance Movement

Battles broke out between those who drank and those who insisted on abstinence. The two sides often fought over licensing laws. Each tavern had to be licensed by the local government to open its doors to the public. Temperance groups, therefore, began lobbying local officials. They urged these officials to refuse licenses to any new taverns. During the 1830s, a new political party, known as the Whigs, arose in the United States. It brought together northerners and southerners who were opposed to the policies of President Andrew Jackson and his successor Martin Van Buren. Many of the Whigs—men such as the Reverend Lyman Beecher—were strong supporters of the temperance movement.

Nevertheless, politicians still relied on liquor to attract voters at election time. In 1840, President Van Buren ran for reelection against the Whig candidate, William Henry Harrison. During the campaign, local political leaders staged events that included plenty of alcohol to win the support of voters. According to one report, "[D]eluges of Brandy, gin, whiskey, and hard cider were poured down the throats of the undecided [voters.]"[4]

Harrison defeated Van Buren. In large part, this occurred because the United States was in a severe economic depression. Many workers had lost their jobs. Some of them abused alcohol. Out of the depths of the depression arose a new temperance movement. In 1840, a group of tradesmen founded the Washingtonians in Boston. The Washingtonians—named after George Washington—were committed to abstinence. They tried to stop alcoholics from drinking. By 1843, one million Washingtonians had pledged total abstinence.[5]

The new movement relied on a variety of techniques to lure workingmen away from drinking. Individual chapters of the Washingtonians established lodges where members gathered. Each member described his own experience with alcohol. The members received support from other Washingtonians in the struggle to remain dry. The friendship and the enthusiasm of the members helped many of them achieve total abstinence. Meanwhile, alcohol consumption continued to fall in the United States. By 1845, it had declined from 3 gallons (11 L) per person to under 2 gallons (8 L).[6]

Groups like the Washingtonians had made abstinence very popular. In fact, a temperance meeting was held in the United States Congress. The meeting proclaimed that ardent spirits were "incompatible with the obligations of social and moral duty, by every patriot and especially by every Christian in the country."[7] One member of Congress, Abraham Lincoln, a congressman from Illinois, delivered an address to the Washingtonians in 1842. Lincoln recognized the dangers of drinking. But he cautioned his audience to consider alternatives to abstinence.

By the mid-1840s, the Washingtonian movement had begun to decline. Conflicts had broken out between the leaders of the Washingtonians and the clergy. Clergymen had traditionally been in charge of the temperance movement. The clergy resented the Washingtonians. For not supporting them, the Washingtonians criticized the clergy as well as the leaders of older temperance societies.

As the Washingtonians declined, other groups took their place. These included the Sons of Temperance and the Good Templars. About 10 percent of the adult population belonged to temperance groups. They included men as well as women. The Martha Washingtonians had been founded to organize female temperance workers. They were affiliated with the Washingtonians and named after the wife of George Washington. Alcohol had impacted many women. Their husbands wasted time and money drinking in local taverns. Members of the Martha Washingtonians brought the message of abstinence to young workers.

Nevertheless, the majority of Americans still continued to drink. In fact, during the 1850s, alcohol consumption began to rise once again. Temperance groups pointed to an influx of immigrants from Western Europe. Many Irish immigrants arrived in large cities such as New York. They continued the tradition of whiskey drinking that they had brought from Ireland. Since whiskey was cheaper in the United States, the Irish could afford to drink more of it. German immigrants brought a taste for beer, a traditional drink in Germany.

As cities grew in size, more and more saloons began to open. The word "saloon" arose from the French word *salon*, a place where people gathered and talked. The saloons were places where people gathered, talked, and drank. Sometimes, too much drinking led to violent brawls and even death.

A Leader Emerges

Born in 1790 in Tipperary, Ireland, Mathew Theobald became a Catholic priest in 1814. He did much of his work in the Irish city of Cork, on the western coast. There he

This photo shows the inside of Hannah & Hoggs Saloon in Chicago in 1889. During the 1800s, saloons became important gathering places for men after work, where they could drink and meet friends and even eat food that was provided by the saloons for little or no money.

helped the poor. Father Theobald recognized that heavy drinking was a serious problem. In 1838, he began a campaign to prohibit drinking. Father Theobald's charismatic personality helped convince more than five million drinkers to take the pledge of abstinence. Theobald led his campaign throughout Ireland. He inspired one hundred eighty thousand people to join him in Dublin, the capital. He also took his temperance movement into Scotland and England. This was part of the prohibition movement that had arisen in Western Europe in the 1830s.

These movements were inspired by the work of the American Temperance Society. The Scottish Temperance Society arose in Scotland. Swedish reformers started the Swedish Temperance Society, which had one hundred thousand members by 1845. Women and children joined these groups. Temperance was also taught in elementary schools.

In 1849, Father Theobald was invited to the United States, where he spoke to thousands of Americans in the East and Midwest. An estimated six hundred thousand took the abstinence pledge.[8] Father Theobald met with President Zachary Taylor and was invited to appear in Congress. In 1851, Father Theobald returned to Ireland, continuing his work until his death five years later.

The First Prohibition Laws

During the 1850s, temperance leaders tried to get laws passed to make liquor illegal. As many as fifteen states, primarily in the Midwest and Northeast, passed these laws. Leading the movement was a short, curly-haired, self-made millionaire from Maine named Neal Dow. Born in 1804, Dow later took over his father's tanning business in Portland, Maine. The business had become very successful. This enabled Dow to devote more of his time to the temperance cause.

Dow became chief of the local fire department. There he continued to promote temperance. The new fire chief did not let the firefighters drink. These were hearty men who enjoyed alcohol. Anyone who violated Dow's order and arrived at a firehouse after stopping at a tavern was ordered out. From Portland, Dow expanded his temperance efforts to the rest of Maine. During the late 1840s, he tirelessly traveled the dirt roads of the state. Dow carried a petition in hopes of getting the Maine legislature to prohibit drinking.

After gathering thousands of signatures, Dow presented the petition to the legislature. A bill introduced by legislators who supported Dow was, at first, voted down. But in 1851, a majority passed a law prohibiting the sale and manufacture of alcohol. Violators would receive fines and prison sentences. This was known as the Maine Law. It was hailed by the Reverend Lyman Beecher. "This thing is of God," he thundered. "That glorious Maine law was a square and grand blow right between the horns of the Devil."[9]

But many taverns in Maine broke the law. So Dow began to lead raids on these saloons. He destroyed kegs of beer and broke glasses. In 1851, Dow was elected Portland's mayor. Voters who believed in temperance supported him.

Dow believed that many larger communities, including Portland, had now banned alcohol. But he may have overstated his own success. Many tavern owners found a way to avoid the law without exactly breaking it. Saloons traditionally offered their customers food, such as crackers or nuts. These were served along with beer and whiskey. Crafty saloon keepers decided to give away the drinks but charge for the food. Selling the drinks was against the Maine Law.

Massachusetts encountered a similar problem after passing a "fifteen-gallon law." This prohibited tavern owners from selling customers anything smaller than a 15-gallon (57-liter) jug of alcohol. The legislators reasoned that this law would eliminate most customers. They only came into a saloon for a couple of drinks. But clever drinkers easily found a way around the law. A group of them arrived at a tavern and purchased 15 gallons of alcohol. Then they took it away with them for a drinking party.

The prohibition laws simply could not stop drinking. Many people found legal ways around the laws. In fact, alcohol consumption increased.

Temperance Declines During the Civil War

During the 1850s, people regularly violated temperance laws, which were not strictly enforced. Much of the enthusiasm for reform in America was channeled into a more powerful movement. Abolitionists throughout the North were trying to bring an end to slavery. Across the South, more than four million African Americans lived as slaves. Abolition leaders, such as William Lloyd Garrison and Frederick Douglass, vowed to destroy slavery. The abolition movement attracted many of the same people who believed in temperance. But the abolition of slavery was a far more burning issue. In 1860, Republican Abraham Lincoln was elected president. He ran on a platform that pledged to stop the expansion of slavery. Soon afterward, Southern states established the Confederate States of America.

The temperance movement declined during the Civil War. Some states repealed their prohibition laws. Nevertheless, prohibition leaders, such as Neal Dow, continued to devote themselves to reform. In 1861, Dow became the colonel of the 13th Maine Infantry regiment. A strict disciplinarian, Dow also insisted that none of his men touch alcohol. Dow's regiment was unusual, however. Throughout the Union and Confederate armies, soldiers received a regular ration of alcohol as part of their supplies. On Civil War battlefields, thousands of men were killed or wounded in a single day. Liquor helped many soldiers deal with the pain of war wounds.

Nevertheless, temperance leaders were appalled to learn that Union General Ulysses S. Grant was a heavy drinker. They believed he set a bad example and should be removed from command. A group of temperance leaders approached President Lincoln. They asked him to fire Grant. Lincoln listened politely to their request. Then he let them know that Grant was the only Union general who won any battles. Lincoln added that he would like to know Grant's brand of liquor. The president said that he intended to pass it out to the rest of his generals.

Temperance Grows Again

After the Civil War had ended, Congress abolished slavery. The temperance movement began to grow once again. Membership in the Good Templars rose from sixty thousand to four hundred thousand by 1869.[10] Four years earlier, the Templars had joined with other temperance groups. They formed the National Temperance Society. This was a loose organization led by William E. Dodge. The society published monthly magazines and hundreds of pamphlets, urging people to stop drinking.

Dodge and his followers hoped to get a lot of people interested in their organization. It was not receiving strong support from either of the major political parties. Temperance split many Republicans—some supported it, while others did not. Democrats, meanwhile, generally believed that an individual's drinking habits were strictly personal. They believed each person should have the freedom to drink or abstain.

Neither political party was prepared to take a strong stand on abstinence. Therefore, temperance leaders started their own political party, the Prohibition Party, in 1869. John Russell, from Michigan, led the party from its founding until 1872. That year, the party ran its first candidates for president and vice president of the United States. In fact, every four years, the Prohibition Party has continued to nominate a presidential candidate. In 1880, Neal Dow was named the candidate for president on the Prohibition Party platform. However, a Prohibition Party candidate never won a presidential election.

Women had also been joining the temperance movement since the early nineteenth century. They had become members of the Daughters of Temperance, which was associated with the Sons of Temperance, during the 1820s and 1830s. However, women were generally denied the opportunity of speaking in mixed groups of men and women. Society believed it to be inappropriate and indelicate.

In 1852, for instance, the New York State Sons of Temperance prohibited Susan B. Anthony from speaking at their meeting. She was a member of the Daughters of Temperance. As a result, later that year, women met in Rochester, New York, and formed their own group. Anthony and others called it the New York Temperance Women's Society. Elizabeth Cady Stanton became president of the society. Both Anthony and Stanton were dedicated to spreading the temperance message. Later, they became leaders of the women's suffrage movement. This movement sought the right to vote for women and included many female temperance activists.

The Movement Gathers Speed

By the early 1870s, the temperance movement began to gather new momentum. A women's crusade had arisen at the grassroots level.

Much of this change had occurred as a result of the Civil War. As men marched off to battle, women stayed behind. They ran farms and businesses and took care of children. Some women collected clothing and material for bandages. These were sent to soldiers. Still others nursed wounded soldiers. Women like Elizabeth Thompson of Hillsboro, Ohio, the mother of an alcoholic son, believed that these experiences gave them the right to join temperance societies. Her husband, a prominent attorney and a former governor of Ohio, was opposed to what she planned. Nevertheless,

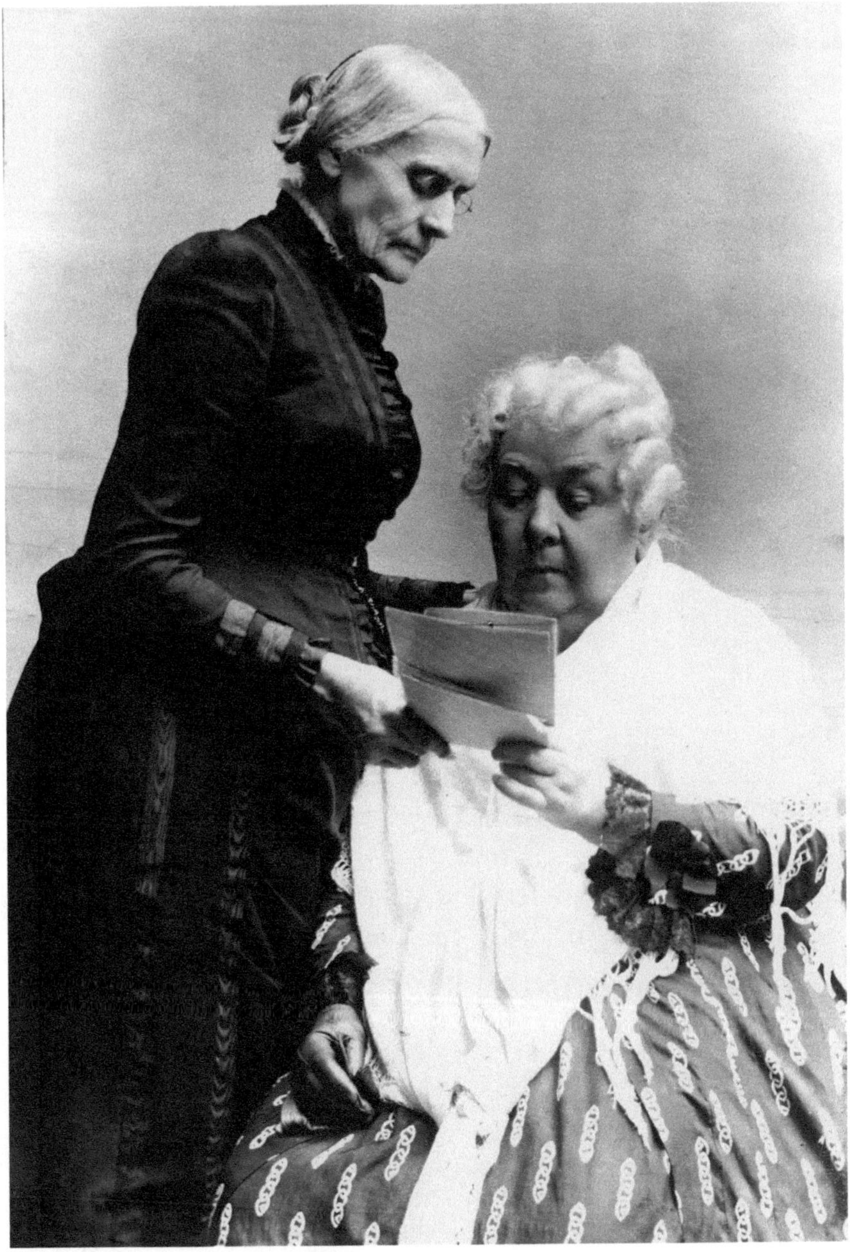

Susan B. Anthony (*left*) and Elizabeth Cady Stanton were among the earliest women's rights leaders who championed the twin causes of temperance and women's suffrage.

Diocletian Lewis

Diocletian Lewis was the first leader of the late-nineteenth-century crusade. His religious beliefs convinced him that prayer could help heavy drinkers reform their habits. Lewis proposed a series of prayer vigils by women in front of local saloons. He believed that customers would be moved by the fervent efforts of women praying for them. This might persuade bar patrons to stop drinking and give up alcohol. Lewis had firsthand experience with alcohol—his father had been a heavy drinker.

The temperance movement was led primarily by women, but a few men also rose to leadership positions, including Diocletian "Dio" Lewis, who believed in the power of prayer to overcome alcoholism.

For twenty years, beginning in the 1850s, Lewis had delivered his lecture "The Duty of Christian Women in the Temperance Work." The lecture had little impact until 1873. Then, Lewis arrived in Hillsboro, Ohio, and Washington Court House, Ohio. In each town, he spoke to a group of women, who were moved by his lecture.

inspired by a lecture titled "The Duty of Christian Women in the Temperance Work" by Diocletian Lewis, Thompson and her friends marched into saloons and taverns, singing hymns, eventually forcing some of the saloons to go out of business.

More and more women joined the effort. They marched in West Virginia, Wisconsin, and Missouri. According to historian Carol Mattingly, as many as one hundred forty-three thousand women took part in more than nine hundred marches, "the largest public demonstration by women in the nineteenth century."[11] Sometimes, they were met with harsh words from tavern owners. People also pelted the women with rotten eggs and bricks and dumped beer on them. Customers inside saloons even covered them with paint. In some towns, children joined the crusade. They asked men in the taverns to take the pledge. As a result, thousands of taverns closed.[12] Elizabeth Thompson and other leaders of the crusade were honored for their courage. For giving birth to this new movement, she was called Mother Thompson.

Unfortunately for Thompson, most of the taverns she closed were eventually reopened. Clearly a more powerful approach would be necessary to achieve lasting success.

4

WOMEN TAKE THE LEAD

By the last quarter of the nineteenth century, the role of women in American society was changing. More women were entering the workplace, mastering a new invention called the typewriter and becoming secretaries. Others had achieved greater independence by learning to ride another new invention called the bicycle. Some women had become active in the suffrage movement, demanding the vote for women, while still others had joined the temperance movement.

Amelia Jenks Bloomer became one of the best-known leaders of the temperance movement. A woman with finely chiseled features, she was born in Homer, New York, in 1818. After teaching school for several years as an adult, she married Dexter Bloomer, a newspaper editor, in 1840. Amelia Bloomer wrote articles for her husband's newspaper. She also joined the temperance movement that was gathering force.

Bloomer saw that women were often powerless in confronting husbands who were drunkards. Divorce was almost impossible for women who wanted to leave husbands who abused alcohol. And, if women were fortunate enough to be granted a divorce, their husbands kept the children.

Amelia Bloomer became a leader of the temperance movement and one of the few women to own a newspaper. But perhaps she is most famous for her unusual pants, which became known as bloomers.

In 1849, Bloomer opened her own newspaper, *The Lily: A Ladies Journal Devoted to Temperance and Literature.* This was the first newspaper in the United States edited by a woman. As Bloomer wrote, "The idea of living with a drunkard is so abhorrent, so revolting to all the finer feelings of our nature, that a woman must fall very low before she can endure such companionship." But rather than wait for the divorce laws to change, Bloomer told women, "We cannot consent to have woman remain silent on the Temperance question . . . Let her work with her whole heart in this cause and, while she demands a law that entirely prohibits the traffic in strong drink, let her also obtain a voice in making all laws by which she is to be governed."[1]

Founding the Woman's Christian Temperance Union

Bloomer's call to action was taken up by the Women's Crusade in the early 1870s. In 1874, this crusade led to the founding of the Woman's Christian Temperance Union (WCTU) in Cleveland, Ohio. At its early meetings, the WCTU recognized the strength and power of women who had participated in the crusade. The first president of the WCTU was Annie Wittenmyer. She told the delegates at one meeting, "The Crusade has shown that the women . . . can face the cannon and the mob."[2] The crusaders were presented with a special quilt, commemorating their courage. At the same meeting, speakers compared the quilt to the Declaration of Independence.

As their motto, the WCTU adopted, "For God, and Home, and Native Land." The members believed that God had called them to lead the temperance crusade. At WCTU conventions, women delegates often read passages from the Bible. While having strong religious beliefs, WCTU members were critical of church leaders. They said that these men had not spoken out forcefully about the problems of alcohol.

Another part of the WCTU motto was "home." Members of the organization believed that they were defending their homes. They did this by closing down taverns where men became drunk. They viewed these taverns as centers of vice. The taverns not only included heavy drinking but also prostitution. These vices threatened the security of homes and families. Women were no longer willing to do nothing. They did not want to remain powerless to stop the activities of their sons and husbands. Leaders of the WCTU reminded women of the active roles they had played during the Civil War; they had defended their "native land," the third part of the WCTU motto.

After the war had ended, women wanted new roles. They did not want to return to a role in which they remained submissive to men. Many men and women felt this was the appropriate role for a woman to play. But the members of the WCTU disagreed. Instead, they planned to make themselves heard on the subject of temperance.

Leaders of the WCTU

Many of the WCTU members were well educated. They came from middle-class backgrounds. Fully half were married to men who were professionals, including lawyers, managers, business owners, clerks, and salesmen. However, a number of the WCTU leaders were single. The WCTU did not permit men to join. Women ran all aspects of the WCTU, including its many publications. They published the organization's newspaper, the *Union Signal.* At first, the organization, under the direction of Annie Wittenmyer, focused only on temperance. They targeted heavy drinking among the poor in America's cities. The WCTU also established reform clubs, where recovering alcoholics met together and tried to help each other stay sober. Members of reform clubs included men as well as women.

During the 1870s, however, the WCTU broadened its activities. In 1879, the members elected a new president, Frances Willard. The charismatic Willard had urged the organization to broaden its appeal. She wanted the WCTU to become involved in other reform efforts.

Willard was a gifted speaker who believed that much broader social problems lay behind intemperance. One of these problems was poverty. More and more immigrants arrived in the United States during the last quarter of the nineteenth century. They crowded into run-down slums in large cities. Willard led a campaign for better wages and shorter workdays. The WCTU also wanted to improve living conditions for prisoners. Under Willard's direction, the WCTU established a Kitchen Garden department. It taught girls from the poor areas how to cook and run households so they could become maids. In this way, Willard and the WCTU hoped to prevent them from turning to prostitution to support themselves.

Willard also allied herself and the WCTU with the Knights of Labor. This was the major labor union in the United States. She supported the right of working people to strike for higher wages and better working conditions. Terrence Powderly was president of the Knights. He supported the WCTU and its temperance message. Powderly was convinced that alcohol prevented many

Frances Willard recognized that temperance was only one of the issues confronting American society, and she urged women to devote themselves to other problems, such as eliminating poverty and poor working conditions.

The Words of Frances Willard

In addition to her work at the WCTU, Willard was also an author. Her works include *How I Learned to Ride the Bicycle: Reflections of an Influential 19th Century Woman*, published in 1895. While many people were opposed to women riding bicycles because their dress seemed undignified, Willard retorted: "An ounce of practice is worth a ton of theory; and the graceful and becoming costume of woman on the bicycle will convince the world that has brushed aside the theories . . . of dress reformers."[3] Among her other books was one aimed at girls, urging them to take a more prominent and assertive place in society. Published in 1887, it was titled *How to Win: A Book for Girls*. Following this book, Willard published *Woman in the Pulpit*, published at a time when the role of clergy was confined to men.

laborers from spending their money wisely on food and housing for their families.

The WCTU organization supported many reform efforts. But it did not forget its primary mission. Willard and her associates established a Department of Scientific Temperance. Led by Mary Hunt, it was aimed at educating children about the problems of alcohol. The WCTU also lobbied, or tried to influence, politicians. As a result, each state passed legislation requiring temperance education in the schools. Children learned a reading exercise that opposed licensing saloons. It began:

> Licensed—to do thy neighbor harm,
> Licensed—to kindle hate and strife,
> Licensed—to nerve the robber's arm,
> Licensed—to whet the murderer's knife.[4]

Many members of the WCTU also took a pledge to marry men who abstained from drinking alcohol. "Lips that have touched liquor shall never touch mine" was their motto.[5]

Willard herself was a tireless speaker. She addressed local chapters of the WCTU across the United States. The WCTU's membership numbered about one hundred fifty thousand by 1890. Willard wore a white ribbon, the badge of the WCTU, pinned to her dress and distinctive pince-nez glasses on her nose. In her speeches, she urged women to work together for temperance. "[We] must stand by each other in this struggle," she told her audiences, "we must move forward, with no break in the ranks . . . and, above all, the bond of peace."[6]

Not only was Willard an effective speaker, she also taught other women of the WCTU to master public speaking as well. The organization was a training ground for women to take a leadership role in public affairs. "Very few could make a speech at that early period," Willard recalled. "We gave speechlets instead, off-hand talks of from five to fifteen minutes."[7] Gradually, the women improved their speaking abilities. They bought publications from the WCTU. These included Willard's pamphlet *How to Conduct a Public Meeting*. Then the WCTU gave women an opportunity to speak in front of church groups and their own local chapters of the union.

The Lure of Politics

The WCTU faced strong opposition from men and women who liked to drink or otherwise did not support temperance. Indeed, the amount of alcohol consumed in the United States more than doubled between 1879 and 1898.[8] Much of the WCTU's efforts were aimed at passing legislation that outlawed the sale of alcohol. Members of the two major political parties, Democrats and Republicans, were divided on this issue. Therefore, Republican and Democrat leaders hesitated to take a strong stand for or against prohibition. Those who did often found themselves losing an election. During the 1870s, the WCTU backed the efforts of Republican Governor John St. John to pass prohibition legislation in Kansas. St. John was eventually successful. But Republicans refused to nominate him for another term as governor.

Willard allied the WCTU with the Prohibition Party to influence state and national elections. But the Prohibition

Frances Willard, among other temperance leaders, believed that only political action would lead to prohibition, so she allied the WCTU with the new Prohibition Party to elect people who would support temperance. Willard (the only woman in the right half of the image) is pictured in this illustration of the Prohibition Party leaders of 1884.

The Prohibition Party Platform

In 1900, the Prohibition Party's platform included the following:

> Few declare that there is no principle now advocated, by any other party, which could be made a fact in government with such beneficient moral and material results as the principle of prohibition, applied to the beverage liquor traffic; that the national interest could be promoted in no other way so surely and widely as by its adoption . . . forbidding the manufacture, sale, exportation, importation, and transportation of intoxicating liquors for beverage purposes. . . . So long as the saloon debauches the citizens and breeds the purchasable voter, money will continue to buy its way to power. Break down this traffic, elevate manhood, and a sober citizenship will find a way to control dangerous combinations of capital.[9]

The Prohibition Party still exists today. Their opposition to the production, transportation, and sale of alcohol has expanded to include tobacco, marijuana, and all other recreational drugs.

Party never became strong enough to have a major impact on politics. Willard's efforts also cost her the support of some WCTU members who did not agree with her decision to ally the organization with the Prohibition Party.

Meanwhile, the WCTU continued to lobby for statewide prohibition laws. By the 1880s, North and South Dakota—as well as Rhode Island, Maine, and Kansas—had these laws. Other states resisted prohibition. The beer and liquor lobbies spent money lavishly on election campaigns. They supported candidates who were opposed to prohibition. At election time, taverns often served as polling places. By offering free drinks and food, tavern owners could sway their customers. As the *Liquor Man's Advocate* put it, "Every saloon averages eighty regular customers and these eighty customers have eighty votes, and, if properly managed, every bartender might influence these eighty votes to a given point."[10]

Many Americans drank alcohol. They also believed that no one had the right to interfere with their freedom to do so. Moreover, conflict had weakened the temperance forces. Willard's alliance with the Prohibition Party had divided the WCTU. The party itself was in conflict over whether to focus only on prohibition or a broader range of issues. Only a few states had adopted prohibition legislation. The time had come for the temperance forces to reorganize and redirect their efforts, if they hoped to achieve success.

5

THE ANTI-SALOON LEAGUE

Lobbyists are individuals or groups that try to influence the decisions of elected representatives. Among the most successful lobbying organizations was the Anti-Saloon League. They began with grassroots work, influencing communities, then they lobbied state legislatures, and finally the United States Congress. Eventually, the Anti-Saloon League was successful in persuading Congress to support a prohibition amendment that outlawed the sale and manufacture of alcohol in 1919.

The leader of the Anti-Saloon League was Howard Russell, a slim, distinguished man with thick, dark hair and a pleasing smile. But behind that smile was a powerful determination to remake America—to change it into a dry nation. Born in Stillwater, Minnesota, in 1855, Russell left school at sixteen. He tried a variety of jobs, including cattle driver and newspaper editor. Finally, he decided to study law in Iowa, after which he opened his practice in 1878. Two years later, he married Lillian Davis, a devout Christian. During the early years of his marriage, Russell experienced a religious conversion. As a result, he left his successful law practice and enrolled at Oberlin College in Ohio to study for the ministry.

Howard Russell was a man with a mission—to make prohibition the law of the land—and he succeeded, step by step, state by state, as founder of the Anti-Saloon League.

While attending Oberlin, Russell worked for a small temperance group. It was lobbying for a local option bill. This would give each town in Ohio the choice of whether to permit the sale of alcohol or to ban it. Russell's efforts were successful. In 1888, the Ohio legislature passed the new legislation. Meanwhile, Russell graduated from Oberlin. He became the minister of a congregation in Kansas City, Missouri, and later Chicago.

Chicago was a rapidly expanding city, filled with thousands of immigrants. Many of them worked in the stockyards slaughtering cattle. It was a dirty, dangerous job where men sometimes got hurt. Russell served as a minister among the meat packers and their families. He often had to deal with the problems of alcoholism. Some of these men drank heavily in the local saloons after a long day in the slaughterhouses. In fact, they spent most of their paychecks on liquor. By the early 1890s, Russell had committed himself to the cause of prohibition.

Origins of the League

In 1893, Russell returned to Oberlin College. Oberlin had promised to fund a new prohibition drive in Ohio. But Russell faced a difficult task convincing Americans to adopt prohibition. During the 1890s, alcohol consumption was on the rise. The major increase occurred in the amount of beer drinking, which had doubled since the previous decade.[1] Americans had developed a strong taste for a light beer, called lager. Lager beer was produced by German brewers. They were among the thousands of immigrants who had come to the United States during the late nineteenth century. At the same time, scientific discoveries had occurred in the techniques of refrigeration. These enabled the brewers to keep the beer fresh. Refrigerated railroad cars meant beer barrels could be carried to cities across America.

Beer was readily available at thousands of local taverns. Indeed, the number of saloons had doubled from one hundred fifty thousand to three hundred thousand between 1880 and 1900.[2] These saloons satisfied the needs of their customers for more than just a drink. They also served cheap meals that workers could afford to buy. Unemployed workers could find out about jobs. Tavern owners were more than willing to cash a worker's paycheck. A customer could enjoy a conversation with his friends after work. He could also find a local newspaper and catch up on the day's events. A tavern might have a telephone. This was a new invention that offered rapid communication, but it was not yet installed in most homes. Some saloons also served as local men's clubs. And elaborate German drinking establishments, known as beer gardens, provided a park-like setting with music and entertainment for the entire family.

Men such as Howard Russell, however, believed that saloons were breeding grounds for alcoholism. Competition among the brewers for saloon business had driven down the price of beer. It had fallen from eight dollars to four dollars per barrel, making it much easier to afford.[3] In order to control the liquor business, brewers began buying up saloons. Each saloon became a "tied house," tied to a specific brewer that supplied it with beer. Many saloons were more than willing to sell out. The price of liquor licenses had tripled since the 1880s.[4] This occurred under pressure from the temperance movement. Temperance advocates, such as the WCTU, as well as local clergymen preached against the evils of drink. This persuaded town officials to take every step available to close down taverns. One approach was to raise license fees.

This drove many saloons out of business.

Russell's ultimate goal was prohibition. But he decided to start with more immediate targets—the local saloons and the brewers. At Oberlin, he formed the Ohio Anti-Saloon League in 1893. Wayne Wheeler was among his first employees. Wheeler was a student at Oberlin who had heard Russell speak on campus. Wheeler was hired to help Russell build support for his organization.

Russell planned to work closely with local churches. Many of them were strong supporters of prohibition. The league sent out printed material to the congregations and urged them to hold antisaloon Sundays. League members appeared at these gatherings. They spread the message of prohibition and raised money from each church. Russell spoke at some of these gatherings himself. Before his sermon, he arrived in the local community and toured the taverns. What he saw formed the basis of his talk about the evils of heavy drinking, which

Howard Russell's brainchild, the Anti-Saloon League, began as a grassroots movement and turned into one of America's most successful lobbying groups. This photograph from the early 1920s shows national officers of the league.

proved very persuasive.[5] Many church members joined the league. According to historian K. Austin Kerr:

"Individuals, members of the congregation, or simply local residents, could become members by signing an antisaloon pledge and by making personal abstinence vows and a promise 'to induce others to abstain' and to work to abolish both saloons and the manufacture and sale of alcoholic beverages."[6]

Russell and his associates gathered funds from local churches. With this money, the league published a newspaper called *Anti-Saloon*. Russell also hired employees. They ran local league operations across the state of Ohio. Known as superintendents, these employees helped organize volunteers. They went door to door spreading the prohibition message. League volunteers helped elect officials in towns across Ohio who supported local option laws that forced saloons to close.

The league also hired detectives to investigate any saloons that remained open illegally. The league then sent this information to local police officials who shut down the taverns.[7] From small towns, the Anti-Saloon League spread the gospel of reform to Ohio's major cities, such as Cleveland and Columbus. Russell hired a Methodist minister named Purley Baker to become superintendent in Cleveland. Baker and Wheeler became top officials in the league.

Russell, Baker, and Wheeler led the Ohio Anti-Saloon League. Meanwhile, similar organizations arose in other states. In 1895, they joined together to become the Anti-Saloon League of America. The new organization was under Russell's direction.

The growth of the league coincided with a reform movement that was sweeping the United States known as Progressivism. The Progressives called on government to clean up city slums, improve working conditions in factories, and reform America's drinking habits. Progressives used scientific evidence to show that alcohol destroyed families. The evidence also proved that alcohol damaged the health of babies born to alcoholic parents. In addition, heavy drinking among men reduced productivity in the workplace and led to absenteeism.[8] Russell received large donations from some of America's leading industrialists. They were worried about the impact of drinking. Among them was John D. Rockefeller, head of the huge Standard Oil Company. Later, Russell received donations from Henry Ford, the automobile maker who wanted to be sure his assembly line workers didn't drink while operating machinery. The reform movement also led state legislatures to pass workmen's compensation laws. These laws required employers to pay their workers if they were injured and forced to stay at home. Employers feared that alcohol might be causing workers to injure themselves. This could increase workmen's compensation payments.

The Anti-Saloon League in Ohio used the funds it collected to lobby the state legislature. The league wanted legislators to pass laws that would apply to every community. This included rural towns as well as big cities. Many small towns supported prohibition. But it was different in urban centers such as Cleveland and Cincinnati. There, thousands of workers drank alcohol after a long day at a hot, dusty factory. These cities had refused to shut down their saloons.

At first, the legislature did not listen to the league's lobbyists. But the league continued to support candidates who backed prohibition. They could be Democrats or Republicans, as long as they agreed with the league. By early

1900, the league had helped elect enough state legislators to provide a majority in support of prohibition. By 1905, the legislature passed a bill, but it was vetoed by Republican Governor Myron T. Herrick.

Although most league leaders were Republicans, they decided to back a Democratic candidate for governor in the upcoming election. Former Congressman John M. Pattison became the nominee of the Democratic Party. In a hard-fought election, Pattison defeated Herrick. Shortly afterward, prohibition became law throughout the entire state of Ohio.

Nearing a Victory for Prohibition

The victory of the Anti-Saloon League in Ohio was a signal to the rest of America. The prohibition forces were rapidly gaining strength. The Anti-Saloon League had spread to other states, using the same tactics to achieve success. Alabama and Tennessee, for example, became dry states as a result of political pressure. In some states, the league worked closely with the WCTU to help achieve reform. And older temperance groups, such as the Good Templars and the National Temperance Society, continued to press for prohibition.

By 1903, Purley Baker had become head of the league. He ran its operation from Westerville, Ohio. Russell had gone to work as superintendent in New York. There, he led the state's prohibition reform movement. The league also opened an office in Washington, DC, run by Wayne Wheeler. Meanwhile, the league ran a large publishing operation, called the American Issue Publishing Company. Led by Ernest Cherrington, the publishing company turned out hundreds of publications, all advocating for prohibition.

Purley Baker

Born in Ohio, Purley Albert Baker (1858–1924) became a Methodist minister who championed the cause of prohibition and the goals of the Anti-Saloon League. First hired as a member of the Ohio branch of the league, he was soon named director of the organization. Finally, in 1903, he became superintendent of the national Anti-Saloon League. Baker recognized that only by appealing to masses of manufacturing workers as well as business owners, such as Henry Ford who could contribute large sums of money, could the League eventually succeed in its goal: a prohibition amendment. He had faith that the League could successfully appeal to manufacturing workers, saying that "they need only to be reached to be won." At the same time, he felt industrialists would recognize that "sober workers are reliable and efficient employees."[9] One of Baker's supporters was S. S. Kresge, a multimillionaire five-and-ten cents store owner, who helped finance the League's Industrial Relations work with manufacturing firms. In addition, Baker also established a communications effort aimed at denouncing the beer and alcohol manufacturers. All of these efforts would eventually prove successful.

In one of its pamphlets, the league claimed, "Liquor is responsible for 19% of the divorces, 25% of the poverty, 25% of the insanity . . . 45% of child desertion, and 50% of the crime in this country. And this is a very conservative estimate."[10] However, the league never explained the origins of these estimates.

By the first decade of the twentieth century, the tide seemed to be running in favor of prohibition. Saloons had been entirely closed down in more than 50 percent of the counties in the United States.[11] Many of these were in rural areas. Saloon closings were much harder to achieve in the populous cities. There, beer and liquor companies lobbied local officials. They also used large amounts of money to support candidates opposed to prohibition. In addition, many immigrants—a majority of whom lived in large cities—were opposed to prohibition.

Nevertheless, the League and other prohibition groups continued to press for nationwide reform. In 1912, these organizations decided to propose legislation in Congress. This called for banning liquor from being transported into dry counties from other states where alcohol was legally sold. The effort in Congress was spearheaded by Edwin Dinwiddie. He was the legislative superintendent for the league in Washington, DC. By this time, the league and its allies had helped elect many prohibition supporters to Congress. They passed the new bill, known as the Webb–Kenyon Act, in 1913. However, the act was vetoed by President William Howard Taft. Nevertheless, Congress overrode his veto, and the Webb–Kenyon Act became law. The new law helped states enforce prohibition. It permitted dry states—those that prohibited the sale of alcohol—to stop liquor from being transported across their borders

Edwin Dinwiddie represented the Anti-Saloon League from its office in Washington, DC, where it could directly influence members of Congress and convince a majority of them to vote for prohibition.

from wet states—those where alcohol was manufactured and sold.

The following year, the League helped to introduce another bill. It called for a constitutional amendment to end the manufacture and sale of alcohol across the United States. Congressman Richmond P. Hobson of Alabama introduced the new bill. Hobson was a retired navy admiral who had fought in the Spanish-American War in 1898. Later, he was awarded the Medal of Honor for bravery in battle. Hobson was a firm supporter of prohibition, and he presented a petition signed by six million Americans in support of prohibition. But the bill lacked the two-thirds majority necessary to pass a constitutional amendment.

In August 1914, World War I broke out in Europe. The Allied powers—Great Britain, France, and Russia—faced the Central powers—Germany and Austria-Hungary. For the next three years, the United States stayed out of the war, while providing support to the Allies. Many Americans were opposed to anything that was associated with Germany. This included drinking beer made by German brewers. Meanwhile, the prohibition effort continued. About 50 percent of the population—more than forty-five million Americans—lived in areas that had adopted prohibition by 1913.[12]

The Liquor Industry Fights Against Prohibition

The liquor industry tried to prevent the prohibition advocates from achieving victory. Passage of prohibition legislation would virtually destroy the liquor business. United States brewers and distilled liquor manufacturers poured large sums of money into the election campaigns of candidates who opposed prohibition. Many local officials favored the sale and manufacture of alcohol. It was heavily taxed, raising money for local government. High licensing fees for saloons were another rich source of government income.

To prevent prohibition, alcohol manufacturers created the National Model License League in 1908, led by Thomas M. Gilmore. The league favored laws regulating the number of saloons and the hours that they could remain open. Gilmore reasoned that these laws would satisfy many Americans. They simply wanted to control, not ban, liquor sales.

Nevertheless, the brewers and distilled liquor manufacturers faced enormous problems. First, in the years leading up to the Prohibition era, they were unwilling to work together. Beer manufacturers were convinced that they could survive by claiming that beer was "a temperance drink," since it was not as strong as distilled liquor. Second, the liquor industry had underestimated the strength of the prohibition movement. The brewers and liquor manufacturers were surprised by the speed that prohibition laws were passed in Congress. This proved to be a fatal mistake.

In the 1916 elections, the league threw its efforts behind congressional candidates who supported prohibition, campaigning in districts across the country. The result was the election of sixty-five new dry congressmen. In December 1917, the Eighteenth Amendment to the Constitution was approved by Congress. It called for prohibition throughout the United States.

By this time, the United States had entered World War I on the side of the Allies. President Woodrow Wilson pressed for approval of a Food Control Bill. This prevented grain from being used in the manufacture of distilled liquor.

The grain was needed for bread to feed American troops. The president was also given authority to restrict the use of grain in manufacturing beer and to lower its alcohol content.

As the war continued, each of the states considered the prohibition amendment. Thirty-six state legislatures had to approve the amendment before it became law. In January 1919, Nebraska became the thirty-sixth state. As a result, the amendment became part of the US Constitution. Later that year, Congress passed the National Prohibition Act. Known as the Volstead Act, it was named for Minnesota

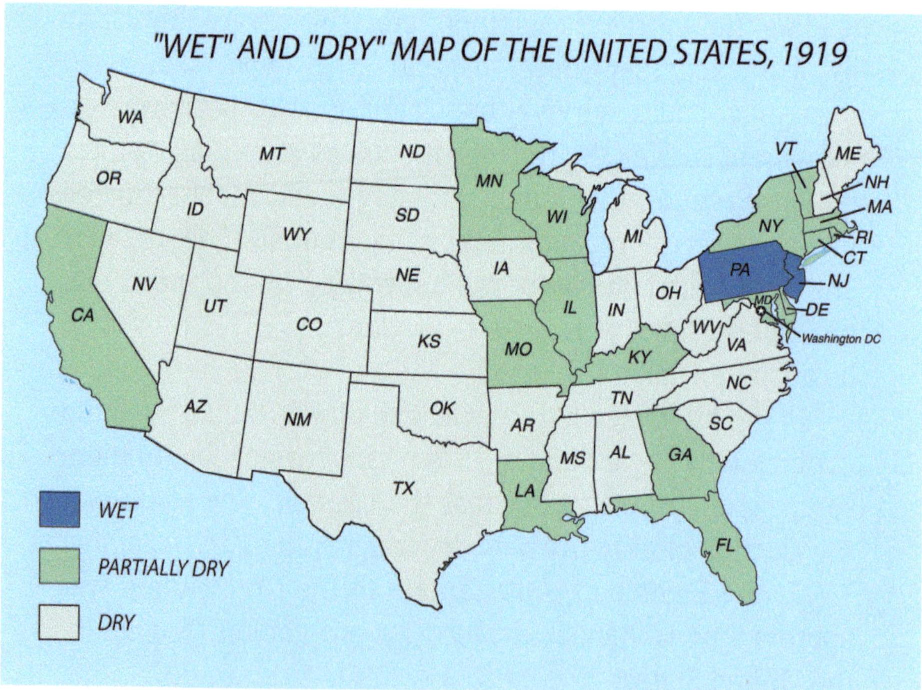

By 1919, New Jersey and Pennsylvania were the only remaining completely wet states. Nebraska became the thirty-sixth state to approve prohibition and make the Eighteenth Amendment the law.

The Goal of the Prohibitionists

Professor Mark Schrad has written that many people think the temperance movement was led by reformers who wanted to stop people from drinking. The real aim, Schrad contends, was not to outlaw drinking but to eliminate the traffic in alcohol. As prohibitionist William Johnson put it: "Any law telling the people what to drink or what not to drink would be overwhelmingly defeated in America. I would fight against such a law myself. . . . But when a man engages in the business of selling what causes such a vast amount of trouble, society becomes directly and acutely affected, and it has the right and the duty of protecting itself. . . . Our laws against selling liquor rest upon exactly the same basis as our laws prohibiting the selling of rotten meat, impure milk or dangerous drugs."[13]

Congressman Andrew Volstead. A lawyer and mayor of Granite Falls, Minnesota, Volstead was elected to Congress in 1903. Volstead was a friend of Wayne Wheeler. Together, they developed the Volstead Act, which slapped large fines and prison sentences on anyone who manufactured alcohol. Any tavern that violated the law was shut down. Any vehicle transporting alcohol would be taken by the government. However, Americans were still permitted to consume alcohol in their homes.

President Wilson did not support the Volstead Act. He vetoed the law, but Congress passed it over his veto. Due to the efforts of such organizations as the Woman's Christian Temperance Union and the Anti-Saloon League, the United States had become a dry nation.

6

THE PERILS AND THE PROMISE OF PROHIBITION

The prohibition amendment promised to end a dangerous problem and remove its effects on the people who drank too much and their families who suffered for it. This was a noble promise, a "noble experiment," as some people said. But the reality turned out to be far different.

Wayne Wheeler had hoped that the new law would contain a provision to prevent the consumption of alcohol. But he was disappointed. The law only prohibited its manufacture and sale. Shortly before Prohibition went into effect, many Americans stocked up on liquor and wine. They hoped this would carry them through the dry years. The law also allowed doctors to write prescriptions for medications containing alcohol. And these prescriptions were routinely written for thousands of patients who liked to drink.

Meanwhile, new shops opened on city street corners. They sold all the ingredients necessary for customers who wanted to make their own liquor at home. These included such items as "hops, yeast, malt…, copper tubing…, kettles…, kegs, bottle tops and other supplies," according

This Prohibition era photograph shows men posing with a large copper kettle still, funnels, and boxes of bottles. The illegal still became very popular among Americans who wanted to drink or sell alcohol to sidestep the prohibition laws.

Reactions to Prohibition

When the Eighteenth Amendment was passed in 1919, one newspaper ran the headline: "U.S. IS VOTED DRY, JANUARY 16, 1919, MOMENTOUS DAY IN WORLD'S HISTORY." William Johnson, an important Anti-Saloon League employee, said, "This is a big moment for me because from this day the flag of my country will no longer float over any brewery or distillery."[1] Reverend Billy Sunday, a leading religious leader, added: "The reign of tears is over. . . . Men will walk upright now, women will smile and the children will laugh."[2]

For the members of the Anti-Saloon League and other supporters of the Eighteenth Amendment, Prohibition seemed to be the fulfillment of all their hard work. But it also proved to be the beginning of an entirely different set of problems.

to historian Eric Burns. There were also recipe books on how to make beer and gin. None of this was illegal under the Volstead Act.[3] Once they bought all of this material, Americans set up their own distilleries, or stills. Others mixed together all the ingredients necessary to make gin in the bathtub. This was called bathtub gin. Gin could be made from alcohol used in industry. This industrial alcohol was still legal under the Volstead Act, although bathtub gin was not.

The manufacture of liquor might be illegal under the Volstead Act, but there were not enough law enforcement officials to stop everyone who wanted to break the law. To enforce the Volstead Act, Congress had established the Bureau of Prohibition. The bureau hired federal agents to carry out the law. Wheeler was convinced that enforcement was the key to the success of Prohibition. He also wanted to control the Bureau of Prohibition. In 1921, he persuaded newly elected President Warren G. Harding to appoint Roy A. Haynes as head of the bureau. Haynes was a close friend of Wheeler's. This enabled Wheeler to run the bureau through Haynes. Wheeler was widely recognized as the leader of the enforcement effort. In fact, he was known as the "dry boss."[4]

To enforce the law, the federal government hired about three thousand Prohibition agents. Part of the agents' job was to shut down every still that was illegally selling liquor. But there were hardly enough agents to shut down every still. In addition, the agents were poorly paid, each never making more than about four thousand dollars annually.[5] The agents were not members of the civil service. That is, they were not required to have specific qualifications or pass a civil service exam for the job. Instead, they were appointed by politicians. As one New York Prohibition official put it, "[Three-fourths] of the . . . dry agents are ward heelers [loyal political party members] named by the politicians."[6]

Because of their low salaries, Prohibition agents were also tempted by bribes. During the 1920s, illegal saloons, known as speakeasies, opened in towns and cities across the United States.

Defying the Prohibition Laws

The speakeasies received their supplies of alcohol through illegal operations. These had started during Prohibition. They were called bootlegging businesses. This term may have originated in the eighteenth century. Many farmers tried to avoid a government tax on alcohol. So they carried the alcohol concealed in the top of their boots. Then they sold it. These farmers became known as bootleggers.

During Prohibition, bootlegging businesses purchased some of their liquor outside the United States. Prohibition did not exist in Europe. Nor did it exist on the islands of the Caribbean, south of the United States. Ships loaded with rum and other types of liquor regularly sailed to North America. Then they anchored off the coast. As long as they remained 3 miles [5 km] offshore, their liquor supplies could not be seized by US authorities. Bootleggers, using fast, small boats, motored out to the ships offshore. Then they stocked up on liquor and headed inland. The coastlines were patrolled by US Coast Guard ships. But there were not enough of them to stop all of the bootleggers. In addition, the bootleggers' speedboats were generally much too fast to be caught by the slower-moving Coast Guard vessels.

Bootleggers also transported alcohol across the northern border from Canada. In Canada, liquor was still legal. Some of

VERMOUTH

Men and women enjoy their forbidden drinks at a New York City speakeasy in 1933. Many people got a thrill out of disobeying the prohibition laws and spending their evenings at illegal speakeasies, which became extremely fashionable, especially among high society men and women in large cities.

Speakeasies

Speakeasies became popular nightspots for anyone who wanted to drink alcohol. Generally, a customer knocked on a door that served as the entrance to a speakeasy. A tiny peephole appeared in the door. A guard looked over the customers to find out who they were. If they passed inspection or knew some of the other guests, they were allowed to enter. Some of the speakeasies were plush clubs that entertained wealthy customers. These clubs had glittering bars, expensive furniture, and fancy food. Harlem, an African American section of New York, became an especially popular destination for well-to-do New Yorkers. In addition to drinks, Harlem's Cotton Club and other nightspots offered music and dancing. But many speakeasies were not posh clubs. They were dark, cheap dives. These were much like some of the saloons that had been closed down at the start of Prohibition. The owners often bribed federal agents and local police. These officials "looked the other way" while the speakeasies did illegal business. According to one estimate, an illegal speakeasy owner spent over thirteen hundred dollars per month on bribes to Prohibition agents and the local police.[7]

it was carried in airplanes that landed on hidden airfields. Liquor was also driven over the border in trucks. Detroit, located in Michigan near the Canadian border, became an important center of bootlegging operations. Some bootleggers set up illegal breweries and distilling operations. They used these to manufacture their own alcohol. Officials seized over one hundred seventy-two thousand illegal stills in 1925. But many more continued to operate.[8]

Among the most successful bootleggers was the gangster Al Capone (1899–1947). Gangsters made millions of dollars from the sale of illegal alcohol during this time, and they used the money to fund some of their other operations, such as prostitution. Capone and other gangsters, including Dutch Schultz (1902–1935), hired gangs of gunmen who defended their operations. Bloody wars regularly broke out in Chicago and other cities between gangs fighting to control the same territory.

The Bureau of Prohibition

Some members of the Bureau of Prohibition were honest, hardworking law enforcement officials. Among them was Eliot Ness, who was born in Chicago in 1903. In 1926, his brother-in-law, who worked for the Bureau of Prohibition, persuaded Ness to join him. Soon, Ness began investigating the activities of Al Capone. Ness put together a group of honest agents who had not been bribed by Capone or any other hoodlums. They staged successful raids on Capone's breweries. The raids were based on information received from tapping his telephones. Capone tried unsuccessfully to bribe some of Ness's agents, but the attempt made headlines in the newspapers. They called Ness and his men "the Untouchables."

One of the unintended consequences of making alcohol illegal was that gangsters such as Al Capone, pictured here, took over the business of supplying liquor to speakeasies.

Eventually, Capone was arrested on charges of income tax evasion. Found guilty, he was sent to prison in 1932. After the repeal of Prohibition, Ness left the bureau and became head of the police force in Cleveland. Later, he was put in charge of the Diebold security safe company in Ohio. Ness died in 1957, just before his book, *The Untouchables*, was released.

The Impact of Violence and Crime

Most Americans—including Prohibitionists—were stunned by the crime and violence caused by Prohibition. This was not expected to happen.

Few Americans were involved in organized crime. But many others thought nothing of buying bootleg liquor. President Harding and his political friends drank alcohol in the White House. It became fashionable for men and women to carry flasks tied to their hips. These flasks were filled with illegal liquor. And a night out at a speakeasy seemed exciting to many Americans, perhaps because they were breaking the law.

Several states, such as New York, decided to end their own enforcement laws. These had been designed to back up the Volstead Act. New York Governor Al Smith was a leading wet. He drank alcohol and believed that Prohibition should never have been enacted. Local courts were clogged with cases involving people suspected of violating the Volstead Act. The problem had become so severe that courts offered special "bargain days." On these days, defendants appeared before the judge. They pled guilty and were given only a small fine. They avoided long jury trials that tied up the courts.

Prohibition Fails to Work

By the late 1920s, many Americans realized that Prohibition was not working. People who wanted to drink were even willing to pay more to purchase alcohol. The cost of a drink had risen since the days before Prohibition. Bootleggers had to pay bribes to police and federal agents as well as salaries for mobs of gangsters. As a result, the price of alcohol rose by about 270 percent during the 1920s. Beer prices rose by more than 700 percent. Consequently, the consumption of distilled liquor increased because it was much cheaper than beer and could be made at home.[9]

But higher prices did not stop Americans from drinking. The 1920s was a prosperous era of enormous consumerism. Americans went on a spending spree. They invested millions of dollars in the stock market. They also bought automobiles by the thousands, fashionable new clothing, and furniture for their homes. Drinking was part of this wave of consumerism.

Wayne Wheeler and the Anti-Saloon League continued to speak out in support of Prohibition. But Wheeler and the league were powerless to stop Americans who wanted to drink. Once Prohibition had passed in 1919, many supporters of the league believed that the struggle was over. As a result, they stopped making donations. Therefore, the league's funds had declined.

Inside the league itself, there was a conflict over the direction it should take in the future. Wheeler and Purley Baker believed that the league should put its efforts behind law enforcement. But Ernest Cherrington disagreed. He realized that a new law would not change America's drinking habits. Cherrington supported law enforcement, but he emphasized education as the way to ensure that alcohol reform worked effectively. He wanted the league to educate church members about the dangers of drinking. He produced many publications to help the churches in this effort, believing that only an educational program lasting many years could produce real reform. After Wayne Wheeler's death in 1927, Cherrington was more able to guide the league's efforts.

But by this time, the league's reputation was on the decline. Many churches had not supported Wheeler's emphasis on enforcement instead of education and had cut off donations to the league.

Meanwhile, strong groups had organized to oppose Prohibition. Among them was the Association Against the Prohibition Amendment (AAPA), founded in 1918. William H. Stayton, a former naval officer, led the group. The AAPA believed that Prohibition was an example of the government interfering with an individual's private life. As Stayton explained, it was "the desire of fanatics to meddle in the other man's affairs and to regulate the details of your lives and mine."[10] As Prohibition began to weaken during the 1920s, the strength of the AAPA grew. This group included prominent business leaders and politicians.

Women had also organized a similar group. Pauline Sabin founded the Women's Organization for National Prohibition Reform (WONPR) in 1929. She was a society leader and former supporter of Prohibition. "I thought a world without liquor would be a beautiful world," she explained.[11] But Sabin said she had changed her mind because so many people were violating the law. An effective organizer, Sabin was also quite wealthy and convinced some of her wealthy friends to support her movement. This increased its impact in the press. Many women joined WONPR, including some

who had formerly belonged to the WCTU. WONPR grew to sixty thousand members by mid-1929 and more than one million by 1932. Sabin and other women wanted to return the nation to temperate drinking habits. They did not want to continue trying to enforce Prohibition.

Meanwhile, the battle to repeal Prohibition was becoming a national political issue. In 1928, Democrats nominated Al Smith, the cigar-smoking governor of New York, as their presidential candidate. Smith wanted to change the federal Prohibition laws. He believed in letting each state enact its own legislation on the issue. Republicans nominated Herbert Hoover. A former engineer, Hoover had a distinguished record in government. He opposed the repeal of Prohibition. Hoover called it a "great social and economic experiment."[12]

The Anti-Saloon League supported Hoover. He won a landslide victory in the presidential election. Republicans then began strengthening the Volstead Act by passing the Jones Act, named after Senator Wesley L. Jones. This new law lengthened prison terms for violating the Prohibition laws. The Jones Act also increased the fines from one thousand dollars to ten thousand dollars. Under Hoover, federal agents arrested

Pauline Sabin is being held up during an April 22, 1932 demonstration in front of the Capitol building in Washington, DC. Ironically, while women had led the Prohibition movement, they eventually found themselves opposed by other women, such as Sabin, who wanted to see the law repealed.

more people suspected of bootlegging. The annual budget for the Bureau of Prohibition went up to $13.4 million. It had been only $4.4 million at the start of the 1920s.

Hoover's support of Prohibition disappointed many voters. They believed that the law should be repealed. The opposition to Hoover grew after the first year of his presidential term. The United States plunged into the Great Depression. Approximately 25 percent of working people lost their jobs. Meanwhile, the Hoover administration did little to put people back to work.

Those who wanted Prohibition repealed pointed out that before the Volstead Act, the legal alcohol industry had employed thousands of people. These men and women might find employment again. But this could only occur if the manufacture and sale of alcohol were legalized. In addition, the government could tax legal alcohol—as it had done before Prohibition. This would increase tax revenues. The money could be spent on programs to help the unemployed. Finally, the government could cut the costs of enforcing the Volstead Act by simply repealing it.

In 1932, Democrats nominated Franklin D. Roosevelt to run against Hoover. Groups such as the AAPA supported Roosevelt, who called for the repeal of Prohibition. A year earlier, Hoover had received a report from a federal commission, headed by former Attorney General George Wickersham. The Wickersham Commission pointed out that Prohibition had only led to open violation of the law. Meanwhile, groups such as the Veterans of Foreign Wars had joined the AAPA in calling for repeal. Roosevelt was elected by a landslide. Soon after taking office, he changed the Prohibition laws. He immediately permitted the manufacture of beer. Congress passed the Twenty-first

Amendment, calling for the repeal of Prohibition. Before the end of 1933, thirty-six states had approved the amendment, which became law.

On December 5, 1933, a headline ran in the *New York Times*, proclaiming, "Legal Liquor Due Tonight; City Ready to Celebrate; Stores to Open Tomorrow."[13] Prohibition, America's great social experiment, was over.

7

AFTER PROHIBITION

Prohibition may have begun as a "noble experiment," but historians disagree over how successful it was in cutting down alcohol consumption. Historian Mark Thornton wrote that Prohibition "was undertaken to reduce crime and corruption, solve social problems . . . and improve health and hygiene in America. The results of that experiment clearly indicate that it was a miserable failure on all counts."[1] Thornton cited statistics that show the amount of alcohol consumed actually increased during Prohibition. Each American drank an average of about one gallon (3.8 L) of alcohol annually in 1918 before Prohibition began. This dropped to just over 0.2 gallons (0.8 L) in 1921, and then started rising. It reached more than 1.2 gallons (4.5 L) in 1929. However, other statistics indicated that consumption dropped from 2.6 gallons (9.8 L) annually in 1915 to about one gallon in 1934.[2]

During Prohibition, however, doctors and hospitals were handing out alcohol in medicines. These were legal under the law. Sales of so-called medicinal alcohol rose by 400 percent.[3]

Nevertheless, the number of people abstaining from alcohol rose during Prohibition. One reason may have been

The Effects of Illegal Alcohol

Makers of illegal bathtub gin included any amount of alcohol they wanted. They also used any ingredients that they could find. The result was that more people became sick from drinking during Prohibition. Irving Fisher, an expert on alcohol use, wrote, "I am credibly informed that a very conservative reckoning would set the poisonous effects of bootleg beverages as compared with medicinal liquors at ten to one. . . . The reason is that bootleg liquor is so concentrated and almost invariably contains other and more deadly poisons than mere . . . alcohol."[4]

There were 1.6 deaths per 100,000 people from alcohol in 1919 as Prohibition began. By 1927, this figure had more than doubled.[5]

the increased cost of drinking. Many people may have also missed the corner tavern. They did not want to drink behind closed doors in a secret speakeasy. In fact, Prohibition brought an end to the tavern as a meeting place for men. After Prohibition, beer became available in cans and bottles. Americans could refrigerate the beer and drink at home.

Meanwhile, during Prohibition, women drank openly at speakeasies. After the repeal, men and women drank together at nightclubs and restaurants. Reports also indicated that young people were more inclined to drink during Prohibition.

A group of women visit a 1932 New York speakeasy. Speakeasies increased the freedom that women enjoyed during the twentieth century, enabling them to openly drink in public; and this continued after Prohibition was repealed.

Failure to Reduce Crime

Prohibition had been intended to cut down on crime, such as prostitution in taverns. But it had just the opposite effect. Large organized criminal gangs took advantage of the Volstead Act. They supplied illegal alcohol. Murder rates also increased during the 1920s. This was partly because of the gangland wars over bootlegging. Prohibition was also expected to reduce corruption. Before the 1920s, the liquor industry had resorted to lobbying and bribing elected officials to win their support. But many members of local police departments and officials in the Bureau of Prohibition were bought off by the bootleggers.[6]

The Long-Term Impact of Prohibition

Prohibition did not eliminate drinking in the United States. Drinking began to increase again after the repeal. To deal with this problem, some states continued to practice prohibition after 1933. Kansas did not repeal state prohibition until 1948. Oklahoma repealed it in 1957 and Mississippi repealed prohibition in 1966. Meanwhile, every state adopted regulations licensing taverns, liquor stores, and restaurants that served alcohol. Liquor sales were restricted to specific hours and days. Alcohol was not generally sold on Sundays. Some counties and communities also kept prohibition laws. As a result, they remained dry, prohibiting the sale of alcohol.

Following the repeal of Prohibition, the Anti-Saloon League disappeared. However, the Prohibition Party continues to run candidates in presidential elections. The WCTU also continues to operate. On its website is a quotation from the Greek philosopher Xenophon, "Temperance may be defined as: moderation in all things healthful; total abstinence from all things harmful." The WCTU continues to focus on the problems created by alcohol. But the organization has broadened its interests to include the harmful effects of tobacco as well as illegal drugs, such as crack cocaine. The WCTU warns young people that tobacco companies are targeting teenagers and trying to persuade them to take up cigarette smoking. As it did in the past, the WCTU emphasizes the dangers of

Alcoholics Anonymous

Where Prohibition failed, an organization called Alcoholics Anonymous (AA) has been far more successful. AA began because of a meeting in Akron, Ohio, in 1935 between Bill W. and Dr. Bob S., both alcoholics. They created a group based on strong spiritual values, self-help, as well as support from other group members. Soon afterward, another AA local organization began meeting in New York, and still another in Cleveland. By 1939, there were a hundred alcoholics who had stopped drinking. That same year, AA published its textbook, which presented a twelve-step method to sobriety. Newspaper articles began to appear, praising the success of AA, and more alcoholics joined. By 1941, following more publicity, AA had reached six thousand members. Branches had also opened in other parts of the world, and membership had climbed to one hundred thousand by 1950.[7] Since then, AA has achieved an impressive success rate in helping members achieve lasting sobriety.

A man tells his story during an Alcoholics Anonymous meeting in about 1950. Since its founding in 1935, AA has helped many men and women recover from alcoholism.

alcohol, warning that it is "toxic to the body" and telling young people that they can die from drinking too much.

Dealing with Drugs

In the late 1960s, President Richard Nixon began the War on Drugs. The War on Drugs is somewhat similar to the Prohibition movement of the early twentieth century. This effort was aimed at prohibiting the sale and use of drugs, such as heroin, cocaine, and marijuana. The federal government focused on eliminating the sources of drugs. Heroin, for example, is produced from a flower called a poppy. It is grown in countries such as Afghanistan. The American government has tried to convince Afghan farmers to stop growing poppies and produce another type of crop. But this effort has been largely unsuccessful.

President Richard Nixon tried to eliminate the sale and use of harmful drugs, but the War on Drugs has not proven any more successful than Prohibition.

Like Prohibition, experts disagree on what to call the War on Drugs. Is it a

The poppy is a popular plant among gardeners . . . and drug cartels. Heroin, made from poppies, is a major source of income for farmers who have refused to give up this widely-grown cash crop.

modest success, a failure, or something in between? Prohibition, on the other hand, was largely unsuccessful. However, it does mark an important era in American history.

CONCLUSION

The law of unintended consequences states that although an individual, an organization or a government may act with the best of intentions, the results of these actions may not turn out the way they were intended. There is no better example in the history of the United States than Prohibition, the dry crusade.

The impetus for Prohibition was very well-meaning. Many Americans wanted to reduce the highly negative impact of drinking alcohol. Some people, especially men, became addicted to drink with terrible results. They wasted their money, endangered the well-being of their families, lost their jobs, and created terrible examples for their children. Women, because most did not do paid work and their legal status was not equal to a man's, could do very little to stop their husbands. The law would not help them, and most could not afford to leave their alcoholic husbands and bring their children to safety.

Women were stuck—a major reason why some, such as Carry Nation, decided to take the law into their own hands. Others joined movements such as the WCTU and tried to pressure local politicians to do something to outlaw the sale, manufacture, and transportation of alcohol into their communities. Eventually, they were joined by powerful lobbying groups, including the Anti-Saloon League, that increased the pressure on Congress to change the law, leading to passage of the Eighteenth Amendment.

What the Prohibitionists seemed to forget, however, is that for the vast majority of people who drink alcohol, the drug is not addictive nor do they inevitably become alcoholics. Drinking has been part of world culture for several millennia. Many people simply enjoy moderate or occasional drinking. And for some, beer and wine are an integral part of their culture.

Many people like to toast celebrations with champagne or other alcoholic beverages. Drinking does not become a problem for most people.

As a result of Prohibition, people who wanted a drink began to defy the law, including the president of the United States, Warren Harding. And a vast network of illegal suppliers were there to provide the alcohol. They paid off the police to look the other way. They also formed vicious gangs that battled each other for control of the liquor trade, and killed many innocent people. To get around the Prohibition law, some American citizens decided to make their own alcohol, often containing ingredients that were extremely unhealthy and sometimes fatal.

These were the unintended consequences of a noble experiment. The cure was far worse than the disease, especially because there were other ways to treat the problem. Treatment programs and organizations such as Alcoholics Anonymous have proven to be far more successful than Prohibition. But from time to time, democracies go down the wrong path; fortunately, they learn from the experience. And the results can benefit everyone.

CHRONOLOGY

1775 The American Revolution begins.

1785 Dr. Benjamin Rush publishes his pamphlet *An Inquiry into the Effects of Ardent Spirits on the Human Mind and Body.*

1789 A temperance group forms in Litchfield, Connecticut.

1794 The Whiskey Rebellion takes place in Pennsylvania.

1808 The Union Temperance Society of Moreau and Northumberland is formed.

1823 The Hartford Female Seminary is founded by Catherine Beecher.

1826 The American Temperance Society is founded.

1840 The Washingtonians begin in Baltimore.

1846 Carrie (Carry) Nation is born on November 24.

1849 Father Mathew Theobald of Ireland preaches temperance in the United States; Amanda Bloomer begins her newspaper, *The Lily.*

1851 Maine passes a prohibition law.

1859 John Brown raids Harper's Ferry, Virginia.

1861–1865 The Civil War rages; the temperance movement declines.

1869 The Prohibition Party is founded.

1873 The women's crusade against drinking begins.

1874 The Woman's Christian Temperance Union (WCTU) is founded.

1878 The Kansas WCTU is founded.

1879 Frances Willard becomes head of WCTU.

1880 Kansas passes a prohibition law.

1895 The Anti-Saloon League of America is founded by Howard Russell; Frances Willard publishes *How I Learned to Ride a Bicycle.*

1900 Carry Nation begins her campaign of "hatchetation."

1903 Purley Baker becomes head of the Anti-Saloon League.

1913 The Webb-Kenyon Act is passed.

1914–1918 World War I rages across Europe.

1917 Congress passes the Eighteenth Amendment, prohibiting the manufacture and sale of alcohol.

1919 Prohibition becomes law; the Volstead Act is passed to enforce prohibition.

1929 The Women's Organization for National Reform is founded.

1933 Prohibition is repealed.

1935 Alcoholics Anonymous is founded in Cleveland, Ohio.

CHAPTER NOTES

CHAPTER 1

Leading a Revolution

1. "Carry A. Nation," Kansas Historical Society, 2008, http://www.kshs.org/exhibits/carry/carry3.htm.
2. Fran Grace, *Carry A. Nation: Retelling the Life* (Bloomington, IN: Indiana University Press, 2001), p. 151.
3. "Carry Nation Quotes," Inspirational Stories, 2019, https://www.inspirationalstories.com/quotes/t/carry-nation/.
4. Grace, p. 158.
5. Grace, p. 168.
6. "Carry A. Nation."
7. Grace, pp. 79–80.
8. Grace, p. 90.

CHAPTER 2

Drinking Traditions

1. "America's Favorite Drink," *History Magazine*, April/May 2006.
2. Eric Burns, *The Spirits of America: A Social History of Alcohol* (Philadelphia, PA: Temple University Press, 2004), p. 11.
3. Burns, p. 23.
4. Burns, p. 25.
5. Burns, p. 26.
6. Mark Edward Lender and James Kirby Martin, *Drinking in America: A History* (New York, NY: The Free Press, 1987), p. 1.
7. Lender and Martin, p. 18.
8. Burns, p. 10.
9. Lender and Martin, p. 46.
10. Lender and Martin, p. 38.
11. Burns, p. 43.
12. Burns, p. 62.
13. Burns, p. 63.

CHAPTER 3

The New Temperance Movement

1. Thomas Pegram, *Battling Demon Rum: The Struggle for a Dry America, 1800–1933* (Chicago, IL: Ivan R. Dee, 1998), p. 18.
2. Eric Burns, *The Spirits of America: A Social History of Alcohol* (Philadelphia, PA: Temple University Press, 2004), p. 79.
3. Mark Edward Lender and James Kirby Martin, *Drinking in America: A History* (New York, NY: The Free Press, 1987), pp. 71–72.
4. Pegram, p. 27.
5. Pegram, p. 27.
6. Pegram, p. 31.
7. Lender and Martin, p. 74.
8. "History of Alcohol Prohibition," National Commission on Marihuana and Drug Abuse, http://www.druglibrary.org/schaffer/LIBRARY/studies/nc/nc2a.htm (accessed April 14, 2019).
9. "History of Alcohol Prohibition."
10. Pegram, p. 47.
11. Carol Mattingly, *Well-Tempered Women: Nineteenth-Century Temperance Rhetoric* (Carbondale, IL: Southern Illinois University Press, 1998), pp. 41–42.
12. Mattingly, p. 108.

CHAPTER 4

Women Take the Lead

1. Carol Mattingly, *Well-Tempered Women: Nineteenth-Century Temperance Rhetoric* (Carbondale, IL: Southern Illinois University Press, 1998), pp. 26, 29.
2. Mattingly, p. 43.
3. "Francis E. Willard, Quotes," *Goodreads,* https://www.goodreads.com/author/quotes/552029.Frances_E_Willard (accessed January 28, 2019).

4. "History of Alcohol Prohibition," National Commission on Marihuana and Drug Abuse, http://www.druglibrary.org/schaffer/LIBRARY/studies/nc/nc2a.htm (accessed April 14, 2019).
5. Joseph R. Gusfield, *Symbolic Crusade: Status Politics and the American Temperance Movement* (Urbana, IL: University of Illinois Press, 1963), p. 85.
6. Mattingly, p. 45.
7. Mattingly, p. 60.
8. Eric Burns, *The Spirits of America: A Social History of Alcohol* (Philadelphia, PA: Temple University Press, 2004), p. 120.
9. "1900 Prohibition Party Platform," Prohibitionists.org, http://www.prohibitionists.org/background/party_platform/Platform1900.htm (accessed April 14, 2019).
10. Mark Edward Lender and James Kirby Martin, *Drinking in America: A History* (New York, NY: The Free Press, 1987), p. 106.

CHAPTER 5

The Anti-Saloon League

1. Thomas Pegram, *Battling Demon Rum: The Struggle for a Dry America, 1800–1933* (Chicago: Ivan R. Dee, 1998), p. 91.
2. Pegram, p. 96.
3. Pegram, p. 94.
4. Pegram, p. 95.
5. K. Austin Kerr, *Organized for Prohibition: A New History of the Anti-Saloon League* (New Haven, CT: Yale University Press, 1985), pp. 94–95.
6. Kerr, p. 93.
7. Kerr, p. 95.
8. "History of Alcohol Prohibition," National Commission on Marihuana and Drug Abuse, http://www.druglibrary.org/

schaffer/LIBRARY/studies/nc/nc2a.htm (sccessed April 14, 2019).
9. "Purley Baker," Alcohol: Problems and Solutions, https://www.alcoholproblemsandsolutions.org/Controversies/Biography-Purley-Baker.html (accessed April 14, 2019).
10. "History of Alcohol Prohibition."
11. Pegram, p. 111.
12. Mark Edward Lender and James Kirby Martin, *Drinking in America: A History* (New York, NY: The Free Press, 1987), p. 129.
13. Mark Lawrence Schrad, "On Prohibition's 100th Anniversary, Here's a Distillation of 3 Myths About the Temperance Movement," *Washington Post,* August 1, 2017, https://www.washingtonpost.com/news/monkey-cage/wp/2017/08/01/todays-the-100th-anniversary-of-prohibition-heres-a-distillation-of-3-myths-about-the-temperance-movement.html.

CHAPTER 6

The Perils and the Promise of Prohibition

1. Eric Burns, *The Spirits of America: A Social History of Alcohol* (Philadelphia, PA: Temple University Press, 2004), p. 187.
2. Michael Woodiwiss, *Crimes, Crusades and Corruption: Prohibitions in the United States, 1900–1987* (London, UK: Pinter Publishers, 1988), p. 6.
3. Burns, p. 192.
4. K. Austin Kerr, *Organized for Prohibition: A New History of the Anti-Saloon League* (New Haven, CT: Yale University Press, 1985), p. 226.
5. Burns, p. 231.
6. Thomas Pegram, *Battling Demon Rum: The Struggle for a Dry America, 1800–1933* (Chicago, IL: Ivan R. Dee, 1998), p. 155.
7. Burns, p. 200.
8. "History of Alcohol Prohibition," National Commission on Marihuana and Drug Abuse, http://www.druglibrary.org/

schaffer/LIBRARY/studies/nc/nc2a.htm (accessed April 14, 2019).

9. Mark Thornton, "Alcohol Prohibition Was a Failure," Cato Policy Analysis, July 17, 1991, https://www.cato.org/publications/policy-analysis/alcohol-prohibition-was-failure.
10. Mark Edward Lender and James Kirby Martin, *Drinking in America: A History* (New York, NY: The Free Press, 1987), p. 156.
11. "Pauline Sabin: Repeal of Prohibition Leader," Alcohol: Problems and Solutions, https://www.alcoholproblemsandsolutions.org/pauline-sabin-repeal-prohibition-leader/ (accessed April 14, 2019).
12. "History of Alcohol Prohibition."
13. "Legal Liquor Due Tonight; City Ready to Celebrate; Stores to Open Tomorrow," *New York Times*, December 5, 1933, p. 1.

CHAPTER 7

After Prohibition

1. Mark Thornton, "Alcohol Prohibition Was a Failure," Cato Policy Analysis, July 17, 1991, https://www.cato.org/publications/policy-analysis/alcohol-prohibition-was-failure.
2. Eric Burns, *The Spirits of America: A Social History of Alcohol* (Philadelphia, PA: Temple University Press, 2004), p. 279.
3. Thornton.
4. Irving Fisher, *Prohibition at Its Worst* (New York, NY: Alcohol Information Committee, 1927), p. 28.
5. Burns, p. 280.
6. Thornton.
7. "The Birth of A.A. and its Growth in the U.S/Canada," Alcoholics Anonymous, https://www.aa.org/pages/en_US/historical-data-the-birth-of-aa-and-its-growth-in-the-uscanada, (accessed April 14, 2019).

GLOSSARY

abstinence The act of refraining from drinking alcohol.

bathtub gin Alcohol made illegally by people in their homes during Prohibition.

bootlegging The illegal manufacture and sale of alcohol during Prohibition.

distilled spirits Alcohol, such as whiskey, made from a distillation process.

dram shop A tavern or bar.

dry Abstaining from drinking alcohol.

dry crusade The effort to make Prohibition the law of the United States.

excise tax A tax placed on a product when it is manufactured.

hatchetation Carry Nation's campaign to break up saloons with her hatchet.

lobby To try to influence lawmakers to vote a certain way on a law.

Prohibition The federal law prohibiting the sale and manufacture of alcohol; also refers to era when this law was in place.

saloon A tavern.

social experiment An effort to change the customs of society, such as the Prohibition law.

speakeasy An illegal saloon during Prohibition.

still An illegal distillery during Prohibition.

teetotaler An individual who abstains from alcohol.

temperance Moderate use of alcohol.

tied house A tavern tied to a local brewery and serving only its beer.

vice A moral fault.

wet Supporting the drinking of alcohol.

FURTHER INFORMATION

BOOKS

Bertovich, Yvonne. *The Story of the Eighteenth and Prohibition 100 Years Later.* Ocala, FL : Atlantic Publishing Group, 2018.

McGirr, Lisa. *The War on Alcohol: Prohibition and the Rise of the American State.* New York, NY: W.W. Norton, 2016.

Rorabaugh, W. J. *Prohibition: A Concise History.* New York, NY: Oxford University Press, 2018.

Stoltman, Joan. *Prohibition: Social Movement and Controversial Amendment.* New York, NY: Lucent Books, 2018.

WEBSITES

History: Prohibition
www.history.com/topics/roaring-twenties/prohibition
Learn more about the Prohibition era.

Ohio State University: Temperance and Prohibition
prohibition.osu.edu/
Read more on the major organizations of the temperance and Prohibition movements and view political cartoons of the era.

Prohibition: Unintended Consequences
www.pbs.org/kenburns/prohibition/unintended-consequences/
Dive deeper into the effects of Prohibition on American society.

FILMS

Al Capone: The Untouchable Legend (1998), directed by Langbein & Skalnik Media.

Prohibition (2011), PBS, directed by Ken Burns.

INDEX

A

abolition, 6–7, 14, 45, 54–55
abstinence, 36, 39, 45–49, 51, 55, 78, 109
Adams, John, 33, 35
Alcoholics Anonymous, 110, 116
American Revolution, 6, 35–36
American Temperance Society (ATS), 46, 51
Anthony, Susan B., 56
Anti-Saloon League, 8, 72–88, 91, 100, 102, 109, 115
Armstrong, Lebbus, 38
Association Against the Prohibition Amendment (AAPA), 101, 104

B

Baker, Purley, 78, 80, 81, 100
bathtub gin, 92, 107
Beecher, Lyman, 43–45, 47, 52
beer, 13, 16, 26–29, 31–33, 36, 47, 49, 59, 71, 74–75, 81–82, 84–86, 92, 100, 104, 107, 115
Bloomer, Amelia, 60–62
bootlegging, 93, 97, 99–100, 104, 107–109
bribery, 93, 96, 97, 100
Brown, John, 14
Bureau of Prohibition, 92, 97, 99, 104, 109
Burke, Major, 19

C

Cain, Kate, 25
Canada, 93
Capone, Al, 97–99
Caribbean, 28, 33, 93
Cherrington, Ernest, 80, 100–101
Civil War, 7, 17–18, 53–56, 63
clergy, 9, 33–35, 44–46, 48, 66, 75
Coast Guard, 93
Continental Army, 34
Cotton Club, 96

D

Daughters of Temperance, 55–56
deaths, 107, 108
Democratic Party, 55, 68, 79–80, 102, 104
Department of Scientific Temperance, 66
Dinwiddie, Edwin, 82
divorce, 19, 60, 62, 82
Dodge, William E., 55
Douglass, Frederick, 54
Dow, Neal, 52–55
drinking habits
  early America, 29–33
  eighteenth century, 33–38
"Duty of Christian Women in the Temperance Work, The," 58, 59

E

Eighteenth Amendment, 85–86, 91, 115
enforcement, 16, 23, 53, 82, 92, 97, 99–102

F

Food Control Bill, 85
Ford, Henry, 79

G

gangsters, 97, 100, 108, 116
Garrison, William Lloyd, 54
Gloyd, Charles, 17–18
Good Templars, 49, 55, 80
Grant, Ulysses S., 54

H

Hamilton, Alexander, 38
Hancock, John, 35
Harding, Warren G., 92, 99, 116
Harlem, 96
Harrison, William Henry, 47
Haynes, Roy A., 92
Hobson, Richmond, 84
Home Defenders Army, 16
Hoover, Herbert, 102, 104
Hunt, Mary, 66

I

immigration, 29, 49, 64, 74, 82
Ireland, 49, 51

J

Jackson, Andrew, 47
Jefferson, Thomas, 33, 35

K

Kansas State Temperance Union, 14, 22, 23
Knights of Labor, 64

L

Lewis, Diocletian, 58–59
Lincoln, Abraham, 7, 48, 54
liquor industry, 84–88
Liquor Man's Advocate, 71

M

Maine Law, 52–53
Martha Washingtonians, 49
Massachusetts, 26, 33, 43, 53
Massachusetts Society for the Suppression of Intemperance (MSSI), 43, 46
Medicine Lodge, 9, 19, 23
molasses, 28, 33–34
Moore, George, 17

N

Nation, Carrie, 9–19, 23–25, 114
National Model License League, 85
National Prohibition Act, 86
Ness, Eliot, 97, 99

P

poverty, 64, 82
Powderly, Terrence, 64
Presbyterian Church, 39, 42
Prohibition Party, 55
prostitution, 13, 63, 64, 97, 108

R

Republican Party, 7, 54–55, 68, 79, 80, 102
Rockefeller, John D., 79
Roosevelt, Franklin D., 104
rum, 28–29, 32, 34, 36, 93
Rush, Benjamin, 36–39
Russell, Howard, 72–80

S

Sabin, Pauline, 101–103
Schultz, Dutch, 97
Scottish Temperance Society, 51
Second Great Awakening, 43
Smith, Al, 99, 102
Sons of Temperance, 49, 56
Southard, Madeline, 14–16
speakeasies, 93, 96, 99, 107, 108
Stanton, Elizabeth Cady, 56
Stayton, William H., 101
St. John, John, 68
suffrage, 22–23, 56, 60
Sugar Act, 33–34
Swedish Temperance Society, 51

T

Taft, William Howard, 82
Taylor, Zachary, 51
temperance education, 66–67, 100–101
Theobald, Mathew, 49, 51
Thompson, Elizabeth, 56, 59
Triangle Trade, 28
Twenty-first Amendment, 104–105

U

Union Temperance Society of Moreau and Northumberland, 38
US Constitution, 8, 84–86

V

Van Buren, Martin, 47
Volstead Act, 86–88, 92, 99, 102, 104, 108

W

Washington, George, 33, 35, 38–39
Washingtonians, 47–49
Webb-Kenyon Act, 82
Wheeler, Wayne, 76, 78, 80, 87, 89, 92, 100–101
Whigs, 47
whiskey, 23, 25, 29, 33, 34, 36, 38, 39, 47, 49, 53
Whiskey Rebellion, 38, 39
Wickersham, George, 104
Willard, Frances, 64–69, 71
wine, 33–36, 39, 45–47, 89, 115
Wittenmyer, Annie, 62, 64
Woman's Christian Temperance Union (WCTU), 11, 19, 22, 23, 25, 62–64, 66–69, 71, 75, 80, 102, 109, 114
Women's Organization for National Prohibition Reform (WONPR), 101–102